СОБРА...

20-го ФЕВРАЛЯ

...Ы ЗНАМЕНИТЫЕ МОСКОВСКIЕ

УСТРАИВАЮТЪ ЛЕКЦIЮ

...И·ОПИСЬ И ЛИТЕРАТУРЪ

1) Аэропланы и поэзiя футуристовъ

...бретенiй на современную поэзiю Пробѣги автомобилей и промёты аэроплановъ, сократившихъ нашу часть и все мiрооформленie. Новая красота о красотѣ.

(съ малетерской снимокъ съ картинъ)

2) Кубизмъ и футуризмъ

...зитамъ современной живописи Критика. 2) Что такое (искусство) живопись 3) Европа. Краткій обзоръ недавнихъ ... 4) Россiя. Образы Бенклевъ, Рѣпинъ, Врубель. 5) Импрессiонизмъ. 6) Ванъ-Гогъ, Сезаннъ, Ма... Краска. 8) Понятiе «фактуры». 9) Кубизмъ, какъ ученiе о Поверхности. 10) Рондизмъ (Искусство живописи)... ...7) Футуризмъ. 11) „Бубновый валетъ", „Сокоъ, молодежи", „Ослиный хвостъ".

3) Достиженiе футуризма

...стоимость 2) Мы въ митрославахъ науки. 3) Взаимоотношенiе силъ жизни. 4) Городъ дирижеръ. 5) Григорьевъ. ...Задача минувшаго дня. 7) Достиженiе футуризма сегодня 8) Русскiе футуристы: Д. Бурлюкъ, Н. Бурлюкъ, Илья ..., Василiй Каменскiй, Крученыхъ, „Лившицъ. 9) Различiе въ достиженiяхъ позволяетъ говорить о трёхъ мандатахъ... 10) Идея футуризма какъ „пѣный" валетъ въ дружбѣ методы человѣчества.

ЧИТАТЬ СВОИ СТИХИ.

...часовъ вечера.

„А", в въ день лекцiи съ 6 час. вечера въ Дворянскомъ Собранiи,

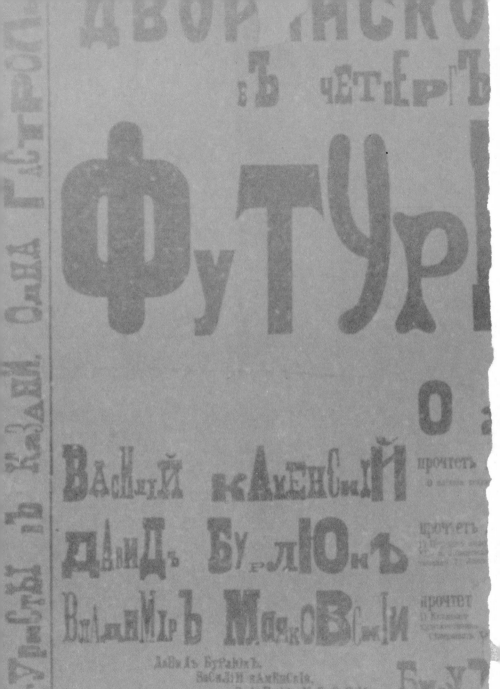

V.MAYAKOVSKY

Vladimir

MAYAKOVSKY

Selected Works
in Three
Volumes

Raduga
Publishers

Vladimir
MAYAKOVSKY

1

Selected Verse

Translated from the Russian
Designed by *Victor Chistyakov*

В. Маяковский
Избранные произведения
в 3-х тт.
т. 1. Избранные стихотворения
На английском языке

Printed in the Union of Soviet Socialist Republics

M $\dfrac{4702010200-175}{031(05)-85}$ 013−85

ISBN 5-05-000017-3
ISBN 5-05-000018-1

CONTENTS

5

Vladimir Mayakovsky, Poet of a New World   7
I MYSELF 29

POETRY

Night 46
Morning 46
From Street to Street 47
What About You? 48
I 48
Great Big Hell of a City 51
How d'Ye Like This? 52
Listen! 52
And Yet... . . . . : 53
War's Declared 53
The Violin—a Little Bit Nervous 54
You! 55
The Way I Became a Dog 56
An Ode to Judges 57
To All and Everything 58
Lily Dear! In Lieu of a Letter 61
Fed Up 63
The Cheap Sale 64
To His Own Beloved Self the Author Dedicates These Lines 66
Revolution (A Poet's Chronicle) 67
To Answer! 72
Our March 73
Clouds Up to Tricks 74
Humane to Horses 75
Order of the Day to the Army of Arts 76
Left March (For Sailors) 77
Ode to the Revolution 78
An Amazing Adventure of Vladimir Mayakovsky 79
Rot 82
Order No. 2 to the Army of Arts 83
Conference-Crazy 85
Paris (Chatting with the Eiffel Tower) 87
We Don't Believe! 90
The Problem of Spring 91
Universal Reply 93
Vorovsky 94
Don't Your Shoulder Blades Itch? 95
Nordernee 98
Komsomol Song 100
Jubilee Poem 104
Vladikavkaz-Tiflis 111
Tamara and the Demon 115
From Poems Devoted to Paris
The City 119
Verlaine and Cézanne 121
Versailles 126
Farewell (at a café) 129
Last Farewell 132
From Poems About America
Atlantic Ocean 133
Some Shallow Philosophy Over the Deeps 136
Black and White 138

Contagious Cargo 140
Topics from the Tropics (en route from Vera Cruz to
Mexico City) 145
Mexico 146
Broadway 152
A Skyscraper Dissected 154
A Decent Citizen 156
A Challenge 159
Brooklyn Bridge 161
Home! 164
To Sergei Esenin 167
To British Workers 171
Talking with the Taxman About Poetry 173
Bribe-Takers 179
A Message to Proletarian Poets 183
A Factory of Bureaucrats 187
To Comrade Nette—Steamer and Man 191
Paperwork Habits 192
The Hooligan 195
A Chat in Odessa Harbour Between s. s. *Soviet Daghestan*
and *Red Abkhazia* 198
Paper Horrors (experienced by Vladimir Mayakovsky) 199
To Our Young Generation 201
My Best Poem 205
Nothing New 207
"Beyond the Grasp of the Masses" 207
Yekaterinburg-Sverdlovsk 210
How Foundryman Ivan Kozyrev Moved into His New Flat . 212
Office-Bugs 215
The Coward 217
Lines Not on Big but Petty Trash. Let Barb-Tongued
Rhymes This Species Lash 220
Crimea 222
Youth's Secret 224
The Pillar 226
The Toady 227
The Gossip 229
Tastes May Differ 231
A Letter from Paris to Comrade Kostrov on the Essence
and Meaning of Love 232
A Letter to Tatyana Yakovleva 236
Conversation with Comrade Lenin 238
Two Competitions 240
All's Quiet in the West 242
My Soviet Passport 244
Americans in Amazement 247
Happy Me! 248
We 250
A Story of Kuznetskstroy and Its Builders 251
Lovers of Hardships 253
Leninites 255
Poems for Children
What Is Good and What Is Bad 258
Meet the Beasts 260
What Shall I Be? 262
Unfinished 268

Notes 293

VLADIMIR MAYAKOVSKY, POET OF A NEW WORLD*

Mayakovsky's work was a phenomenon of tremendous magnitude, with far-reaching effects on the entire development of artistic culture in the twentieth century. The heritage of this outstanding master of socialist art includes lyric verse and satire, long poems and plays, prose essays and critical articles, advertisement rhymes and drawings. And yet the true greatness of Mayakovsky lies not in the scope of his creativity, nor in his equal familiarity with the secrets of the poetic craft and the laws of the stage, nor in his deftness with the essayist's pen and the artist's paintbrush. First and foremost, he was a poet, and as such came to stay in the minds and hearts of millions.

On many occasions, Mayakovsky has been called a "poet-tribune", which, to say the least, is sufficiently justified. His poetry, dealing with many major events and problems of his day, gave powerful voice to the new epoch that saw the preparation and accomplishment of the proletarian revolution. The truly epic sweep of his poetic similes, the audacious novelty of his metaphors, the astonishing force and weight of his poetic rhythms combine in his work with the passion of a publicist, throbbing inspiration and authentic pathos. An outstanding characteristic of Mayakovsky's poetry is its civic outspokenness—by its very nature, it appeals to mass audiences.

In the poem *Aloud and Straight*, to a considerable extent the sum total of his entire life and work, Mayakovsky called himself "an agitator, brazen-mouthed ring-leader", frankly admitting: "I'm unaccustomed to caress the ear with words". But although this poetic acknowledgment has its share of truth, the gamut of his verse cannot be reduced to merely agitator-and-orator-type intonations; it also abounds in the intimate tones of love-confessions, tragic near-shrieks, expressions of sadness, sorrow, as well as caustic irony and good-natured humour. In other words, Mayakovsky's poetry is not only multiform generically, but shows a wealth of colour in its harmonic, intonational composition.

But regardless of the form adopted by Mayakovsky's poetic reasoning, the lyric element is determinative in his work. This quality of Mayakovsky's talent was most precisely expressed by Anatoly Lunacharsky, a prominent Soviet public figure, brilliant essayist and literary critic. On hearing Mayakovsky's recital of the poem *It* in winter 1923, he remarked: "I knew it before but today I have become finally convinced: Volodya is a lyric poet, a most subtle lyric poet, although even he himself doesn't always understand it. A tribune, agitator and at the same time a lyric poet."

In lyric poetry the objective world is reflected mainly through the author's emotions: the events and phenomena of life usually appear here as imprints of these events, as spiritual responses to them aroused in the author.

This fully refers to Mayakovsky's works. Whatever they are devoted to—class battles, travels abroad or debates on art—the poet's attitude to events and facts urging him to take up the pen is expressed with such emotional force and passion, that the poetic structure acquires inimitable, unique features. An account of diverse phenomena of life is combined in such works with an expression of the poet's own thoughts and feelings, with the disclosure of his inner world, the author's "I".

"My time and myself"—so Mayakovsky defined the subject of the poem *Aloud and Straight*. These words could be the epigraph to Mayakovsky's entire poetic output, so exactly do they convey the nature of his verse, combining epic breadth and lyric penetration.

However paradoxical it may sound, in his poems and public appearances Mayakovsky made frequent attacks against lyric poetry. "Lyrics have had from us many a battering," he wrote in his "Jubilee Poem". Especially acid were his remarks about love-verse. "Rhymes to whose sound folks fell in love" he contrasts to "lines to whose thunder Denikin fled from Oryol". His passionate invectives, of course, cannot be seen as a negation of lyricism as such. In the same "Jubilee Poem" the poet confessed:

> But poetry's
> > a damn stubborn thing:
> it's there
> > and it can't be destroyed—that's a fact.

Mayakovsky's critical view of certain forms of lyric poetry stemmed from different sources, primarily, from the awareness that the limits of "old" lyric poetry with its traditional themes of love and nature, with philosophic musings over life, were far too narrow for the enormously complicated world of the twentieth century. The emotional experience of contemporary man, his personal life were connected through numberless threads with major historic happenings. Mayakovsky's attacks on lyric verse likewise expressed his protest against the subjective and spiritless in poetry, against the apology of decadent moods, and manners, which their apologists justified by the inherent right of poets to self-expression.

Mayakovsky felt the need to extend the boundaries of lyric poetry, which complied with the objective demands of his time and his own inner build-up. Indeed, poetry as the "universal sensor" of the epoch could not fail to register the new trends, nor to take into account the fact that in the twentieth century the influence of history in the larger sense, of major social processes on the destinies of separate individuals, on the private life of people, had immeasurably increased.

Mayakovsky became the creator of poetry of a new type, which encompassed political and social reality as never before. In Mayakovsky's lyric verse, history, politics, love and private life—all feature not as a remote background, but as the main object of poetic depiction, the main theme of poetic meditations.

The imminent new epoch would demand new means of verbal expression. The foresense of coming social upheavals and the appearance of new features and properties in literature was extremely widespread in the early twentieth century, particularly in post-revolutionary years. Yet what precisely would those new means of expression be? The answer to this question was interpreted differently. Some writers began to look for it along the lines of predominantly formal solutions. In general, the twenties in Soviet literature witnessed no dearth of artistic "leftism" which claimed to be innovative, but this was never destined, however, to exceed the bounds of formal experiment.

As regards Mayakovsky, his experience in this respect is extremely instructive. The poet more than once permitted himself sharp lounges at classic literature, yet could not bypass its lessons in his own poetical quests. Essentially speaking, his innovations are an expression in new conditions of a number of major features historically evolved by Russian poetry, such, in particular, as its acute interest towards the key social and spiritual issues of its time, militant civic spirit, impassioned publicism. The heritage of many Russian poets and prose-writers—Pushkin, Lermontov, Derzhavin, Nekrasov, Blok, Gogol, Dostoyevsky—was echoed and revived in converted form in Mayakovsky's work. Mayakovsky's innovations and his creative interrelationships with the legacy of Russian classics (very differently regarded by him at various stages of his evolution—occasionally, even negatively) are essentially interconnected phenomena.

One of the salient features of Mayakovsky's poetry is that he regards major social phenomena as if they personally affected him, the writer Mayakovsky.

So, in the poem *Fine* he speaks about the fusion of his own destiny with the destinies of the Revolution, the country, the heroic process of creating a new life:

> *This is time*
> > *humming taut*
> > > *as a telegraph wire,*
> *My heart*
> > *alone*
> > > *with the truth,*
> > > > *whole and sole.*
> *This happened—*
> > *with fighters,*
> > > *with the country entire,*
> *in the depth*
> > *of my own soul.*

In these words Mayakovsky formulated one of the fundamental principles of his esthetic system, affirming the unity between his "I" and the feelings and moods of the people.

On the other hand, he managed to depict his own sensations called forth by deeply personal circumstances, or in other words, facts of a purely personal nature in such a way that they are accepted as a particle of the mainstream of human history full of dramatic collisions, contradictions and struggle.

In other words, Mayakovsky's lyric poetry at the peak of his maturity is also essentially epic, whereas his epic works, including numerous short pieces and long poems, e. g., *Vladimir Ilyich Lenin* and *Fine!* are permeated throughout by intense soul-lifting emotion.

What gave Mayakovsky's work such extraordinary scope, such an enormous power of attraction? What was it that inspired the poet, gave birth to stanzas which are read and re-read today by people of widely different countries and generations? In other words, what are the life-sources and ideas which nourished Mayakovsky's poetry?

Some are inclined to see the mainspring of the poet's magnificence in the wealth and poignancy of his expressive arsenal. Indeed, Mayakovsky was an outstanding master of the poetic word, a reformer of verse-writing. He enriched the poetic vocabulary, introduced new principles of rhyming, new metres, increasing the expressive power and conceptual capacity of each phrase, arranging his verse in step-shaped stanzas. Yet these innovations do not cover by far the concept of Mayakovsky the innovator. The crux of his contribution to poetry lies elsewhere.

Mayakovsky threw in his poetic plight with the historic movement which led to radical social transformations in the world. Acceptance of the ideas of socialist revolution, comprehension of the meaning of revolutionary transformations, became the major formative factors in his work. From them he acquired internal freedom, drew inspiration and obtained arguments confirming the rectitude of his poetry. Mayakovsky's genuine significance lies in that he was one of the world's first writers to link poetry with the ideas of socialist revolution.

Mayakovsky's poetry went through an extremely complex evolution, embodying the evolution of the poet's method and style, the changes in his world outlook. His debut took place in 1912, with the publication of the poem "Night". Immediately, the outstanding features of his talent became obvious. Mayakovsky's early pieces reveal rhythmic intensity, striking poetic similes, as well as unusually vivid imagery. "The crowd—a big tabby-cat, brindled and nimble..." ("Night"), "The sullen rain cast a glance askance...", "The petty wars of the bouquet of boulevard whores..." ("Morning"), "The boats suckled in their entrance-cradles the teats of iron mother-ships..." ("Harbour"), "...with just a drainpipe for a flute..." ("What About You?")—these and many other images and metaphors astound us with their unusualness, a bold combination of completely divergent notions into a poetic whole, leaving an indelible imprint on the memory by amazingly precise portrayal of various features of reality seen by the poet at an entirely unusual angle.

But these were not the only striking aspects of poetic talent exhibited by the early Mayakovsky! His poems of that time are replete with intense suffering, melancholy, tragic reflections.

> *I'm lonely as the only eye remaining*
> *upon the face of one about to join the blind!*

with such a bitter exclamation he concluded the poem "I" written in 1913. With varying intensity the theme of loneliness also sounds in other pieces written later: "Listen! ", "Fed Up", "The Violin—a Little Bit Nervous", "The Cheap Sale", etc.

> *But where's*
> *someone like me to dock?*
> *Where'll I find a lair?*

—this question, addressed to the entire world in the poem "To His Own Beloved Self the Author Dedicates These Lines" (1916), is charged with pain and forsakenness.

Even in love Mayakovsky's hero cannot find refuge. He longs for an enormous, all-embracing love—nothing short of it. But even when he finds his love, the hero still remains alone and unhappy. His feelings are debased, defiled by the effects of the society of private ownership. In his poem *Cloud in Pants* the object of his passion rejects him for the sake of philistine well-being. Similar motifs sound in the poem *Man*, which crowns Mayakovsky's entire pre-revolutionary work. His beloved "wallows in hypocrisy", selling herself to the Lord of All. Nothing remains for the poet but stoic, eternal suffering:

> *When all will perish,*
> *swept away,*
> *He*
> *to whom life conforms*
> *from the last suns*
> *the last weak ray*
> *will burn*
> *o'er planet swarms,*
> *then,*
> *only sharper still my pain,*
> *beside,*
> *below,*
> *above—*
> *I'll stand,*
> *wrapped in undying flame—*
> *unfanciable love.*

There is no place for true love in this ugly world—such is Mayakovsky's final conclusion.

The poet's lyric hero strives to overcome his loneliness. He yearns towards people, hoping to find sympathy and support in them. "For a single word, tender and humane" he is prepared to give away all the treasures of his soul. But he is disappointed: nobody needs nor understands him. Around him mills a "faceless crowd", a "bull-featured mass". In the poem "The Way I Became a Dog" Mayakovsky in sharply grotesque form expresses the idea of the total hostility of the lyric hero's environment; driven to desperation by the bestial mob, he turns into a dog.

The lyric hero of early Mayakovsky shows features of rudeness, even cynicism. Thus, in the poem "A Warm Word to Certain Vices" the poet "glorifies" the might of "the ruble", "sneers" at those who work, "welcoming" blackmailers and card-sharpers. But all this is just make-belief cynicism; the poem is full of hidden pain, tragic irony. Mayakovsky assumes the pose of a cynic and fop out of profound despair, exhausted by eternal solitude, by his confrontation with the "giant bulk" of evil, with the world of petty-bourgeois interests. The poet's efforts to tease and to shock conceal his tragic view of life. It is noteworthy that having assumed such a pose, the poet very soon renounces it. He discards all his teasing masquerade, which is essentially alien to his world outlook, revealing a spirit full of compassion and love for people.

The conflict between the poet and his environment, initially revealed as the lyric hero's estrangement from the hostile mob, rather soon assumes clear-cut social features. Extremely manifest in this respect are the distinctions between the poems "How d'Ye Like This?" and the pamphlet "You", written a year and a half later. In the former the petty-bourgeois whom the poet derides, are identified by purely external characteristics: the crowd is "a myriad-headed louse", "Now you there, Mister, your whiskers still carry the cabbage", "now you there, Madame, ... like an oyster from the shell of things you peep! " The pamphlet "You", contrariwise, has a clearly pronounced political colouring. Mayakovsky exposes not philistines in general, but those who profit from the war:

> *Do you realize, multitudinous nonentities*
> *thinking how better to fill your gob,*
> *that, perhaps, just now Petrov the lieutenant*
> *had both his legs ripped off by a bomb?*

In Mayakovsky's early poems the crowd is totally hostile to the lyric hero. Not finding support and help in the present, he is compelled to seek them in the future. Hence his frequent appeals to "future people", as, for example, in the poem "To All and Everything":

Men of the future!
Who are you?
I must know. Please!
Here am I,
all bruises and aches,
pain-scorched...
To you of my great soul I bequeath
the orchard.

With the strengthening of social motifs in Mayakovsky's poetry, the image of the environment becomes more differentiated. The poet looks for allies in the present. This is especially noticeable in his long poems written directly before the Revolution, in particular, *Cloud in Pants*; the poet not only exposes "lovers of sacrilege, crimes and slaughter", but looks for people prepared to respond to his call for revolutionary rebellion:

Come!
Let Mondays, Tuesdays and Wednesdays
Be dyed by our blood into holidays!

In general, the essence of his esthetic views in those years, the sharp tenor of some of his pronouncements and judgements on art and some of the features of his stylistic manner may be understood correctly only if one considers his relationship with Russian futurists. Russian futurism, which, incidentally, had very few points of convergence with Italian futurism, was far from homogeneous. Mayakovsky was associated with the group of cubo-futurists, whose nucleus was represented by David Burlyuk, Vassily Kamensky and Velimir Khlebnikov. Participating in the public appearances of this group, publishing his verse in futurist editions, putting his signature under corresponding declarations and programme statements, Mayakovsky considered futurism to be a progressive phenomenon. In those years, it was for him almost the only force combatting the customs and art of bourgeois society. Mayakovsky neither saw nor realized at that time that futurism, propounding a subjective and idealistic attitude towards life, history and art, was in itself an expression of the crisis of bourgeois society and was in essence a pseudo-innovative, pseudo-revolutionary trend in art. Mayakovsky's early poems with their tragic view of life, their mounting social protest and deeply humanistic content sharply differed from works following a strictly futuristic line, for the main content of the futurists' poetic activity (at any rate that of most of them) was determined by the desire just to say something contrary to commonly held beliefs. His connection with futurism undoubtedly left an imprint on Mayakovsky's evolution, but, as his further progress shows, it was not strong enough to muffle the social and humanistic pathos of his art. Mayakovsky's enormous talent did not fit into the Procrustean bed of futurism, and his ideological and esthetic evolution brought the poet out onto the mainroad of sweeping artistic generalizations.

The First World War became a major testing ground for many literary and artistic trends and schools, revealing their general essence, exposing their true attitude towards the interests of the nation and the needs of the people. It opened Mayakovsky's eyes on a great many things. He became particularly aware of the fact that the monarchy and the bourgeois system which plunged the people into the abyss of innumerable sufferings was completely rotten. The critical trend in his work gained power. This is well seen in such poems as "Mother and the Evening Killed by the Germans", "I and Napoleon", the pamphlet "You", satyrical "hymns", and especially the big poem *Cloud in Pants*, which presents a major landmark in the development of the poet's ideological self-awareness.

This poem, maximalistic in programme, intensely expressive in style, tragic in the final intonations of the narrative, evidenced the appearance of a number of new traits in the poet's view of life. So, the masses of the people, "the street thousands" in this poem are not merely "sweaty, submissive", their "souls are gold mines", they "hold in their fists the transmission belts of worlds". From behind the wayward convolutions of his poetic thinking, the riotous wealth of his metaphors, in sharp relief appears the pathos of surrounding social life—at times immensely intensified, reaching the utmost breadth of generalization. "Away with your love! ", "Away with your art! ", "Away with your system! ", "Away with your religion! "—so Mayakovsky formulated the main ideas of his poem. And although it still voices the old themes of loneliness, martyrdom, tragedy, Mayakovsky turns towards exposure of the central evil. It is also worthy of note that despite the tragic tone of stanzas concluding *Cloud in Pants*, the poem is not pessimistic. The expectation of new times, a presentiment of change is what determines its poetic atmosphere, its tonality.

Mayakovsky's pre-revolutionary poetry is full of sympathy and passionate, at times torturous love for man crippled by the savagery of the capitalist system. With the years it shows mounting confidence that life must change for the better, that justice must ultimately triumph in this world, that a time will come when such eternal attributes of human existence as greed, cruelty and violence will dissolve into limbo.

> And he,
> the free man
> of whom I holler,
> he'll come,
> believe me,
> he'll come,
> for sure!

This inspired hymn in praise of future man concludes the long poem *War and the World*, where after the first four chapters, immensely impressive in the exposure of the horrors of war, there ensues a picture of universal brotherhood, unity and happiness of all people, projected into the future.

Thus, under the influence of shifts in the general atmosphere of life, essential changes take place in Mayakovsky's poetry. From motifs of loneliness to triumph over loneliness, from exposure of philistinism to an appeal for common people to take "in their fists the transmission belts of worlds"; from epatage, rebellion and protest against the bourgeoisie to the awareness of the need for revolutionary action—such, in essence, was Mayakovsky's mental evolution in pre-October years.

Characteristically, in a number of Mayakovsky's works dated from 1915 to 1917, protest against bourgeois life-principles is accompanied by the expectation of approaching revolution.

> *Where, curtailed, the eyes of mortals halt,*
> *at the head of starving hordes,*
> *I espy*
> *crowned with the thorns of revolt*
> *the year 1916 draws nigh...*

the poet prophesies in his poem *Cloud in Pants*. Gradually, Mayakovsky's poetry gets rid of the feeling of bitterness; motifs of forsakenness disappear, although, as testified by the poem *Man*, he is still not quite able to overcome his tragic view of reality. And yet the expectation of undreamed-of changes seizes the poet with growing strength.

> *Today topples your thousand-year-old Before.*
> *Today the foundations of worlds are revised.*
> *Today,*
> *to the very last coat-button, you're*
> *to start remodelling everyone's lives...*

he exclaims in the poem "Revolution (A Poet's Chronicle)" written in the beginning of 1917. Thus, the theme of revolution, dimly contoured, as it were, in his pre-October verse, becomes central in his entire work.

This evolution in Mayakovsky's stand is explained not only by changes in the general atmosphere of life. It was also prepared by many circumstances of his personal life. Already in his teens he took part in the revolutionary movement, was acquainted with revolutionary literature, carried out the assignments of the Bolshevik Party, spread revolutionary leaflets. He was arrested three times, only his young age saving him from prolonged imprisonment. Although Mayakovsky abandoned direct participation in the revolutionary movement, as he stated himself, "broke off Party work", he always retained his ideological sympathies.

There is a widely known passage in "I Myself"—Mayakovsky's autobiography—in which he expressed his attitude towards the October Revolution: "To accept or not to accept? There was no such question for me... My Revolution." The Revolution, in essence, marked the beginning of the poet's second birth. From then on the Revolution was the main hero of Mayakovsky's poetry. In it he sees the beginning of all beginnings. For him the Revolution is the symbol of liberty and justice, a source of joy and inspiration. As if a mighty explosion, it sweeps away everything that is old and outdated in life.

In his play *Mystery-Bouffe*, written for the first anniversary of October 1917, the Revolution is pictured as a deluge, purging the world of the "heritage" of the old system. The poet shows that revolutionary battles not only destroy governments, but break up the old way of life, change people's customs, feelings and tastes.

October opens a new page in Mayakovsky's work. With it begins the most fertile and significant period in his activity. Yet this does not mean that Mayakovsky's progress towards the heights of socialist art was simple and smooth. More than once under the pressure of life he had to revise his creative experience, his views. He found in himself the strength to reject much that had earlier attracted him by its seemingly revolutionary spirit and novelty. Mayakovsky indulged in an intensive search, occasionally falling into extremes, for new forms of art corresponding to the demands and spirit of the revolutionary epoch.

The Revolution gave vast scope to Mayakovsky's lyric sentiment. It is hard to name any more or less significant event of that time which evaded the poet's attention, which did not arouse his passionate poetic response. It will be no exaggeration to say that Mayakovsky's lyric poetry absorbed all that was most important in the turbulent life of the twenties. The Civil War with its victories and privations, the famine on the Volga, the struggle with economic ruin, the attempts of capitalist states to strangle the young Soviet state, the Genoese Conference, the fight against religious stultification, hooliganism, drunkenness, philistinism, the labour exploits of the people building socialism, disputes about the condition and tasks of Soviet art—all this and much, much more found reflection in Mayakovsky's poetry. His lyric verse presents a unique artistic chronicle of the first thirteen heroic years in the life of the country. It depicted not only the most important events, but the entire spiritual atmosphere of that great and unforgettable time.

In these years, it should be noted, Mayakovsky's lyric poetry did not stay unchanged, but developed, enriching and perfecting itself. His lyric works of the first revolutionary years were still far from concrete realistic portrayal of the new actuality. Cosmic in scope, the images of many of his poems of that time (e. g., "Astounding Facts", "We're Coming") expressed merely the general spirit of the time, its heroic atmosphere, the readiness of the working masses for unheard-of exploits, their confidence that the cause of the Revolution would soon triumph throughout the world, and a new fantastically wonderful life would immediately arrive for all people.

Simultaneously, Mayakovsky's poetry of that period was marked by certain illusory notions. It seemed to him that the Revolution, altering the social basis of life, carrying out a reassessment of many historic and cultural values, rejects as unnecessary and less important than direct revolutionary action everything which people confront in usual life: nature, historic and cultural traditions, the age-old foundations of everyday life.

> *Whose heart's*
>> *been washed by October storms*
> *won't need*
>> *either sunsets or roaring oceans,*
> *won't need*
>> *climatic or natural charms,*
> *nothing at all*
>> *but you—Revolution!*

The poet called on his audience to "wipe out the old" from their hearts, "not only, building the new, to fantasize, but to dynamite the old", "run down old History's hack". He insisted that "it's time for bullets to whizz through museums", that Nature wasn't worth "absolutely anything", etc. The poet was inclined to view art only in the concrete, utilitarian sense. Mayakovsky believed that on the background of grandiose revolutionary transformations carried into effect by the activity of millions, the efforts of the human individual were dissolved in the actions of these millions, i. e., the individual was completely absorbed by the collective. Hence the poet's desire to somewhat damp down his lyric sentiment, which is apparent in some of his works, particularly, the poem *150,000,000*, written in early 1920. With sweeping epic strokes of his pen, the poet depicts the image of many-faced Russia aroused by the Revolution. He shows the indomitable power of the millions united in a single drive to "dynamite" the old world. But in this image there is more of elemental power than orderly force, organized and guided by the Party.

> *Not for Lenin endearing verse comes from me.*
> *But for millions in battle.*
> *The millions I sing,*
>> *the millions I see,*
> *for the millions*
>> *my lyre-strings rattle.*

Such unqualified glorification of "the millions" alone appears somewhat too biased in favour of the masses, as opposed to the individual. The spirit of anonymity, permeating the poem, was detrimental to the image of the people which it depicted. The poet, as it were, shackled his lyric feeling, not letting it reveal itself to the full.

Of course, many of the mentioned poetical assertions, which in part bore the imprint of futurist theories, should not be taken at their face value. Doubtlessly, they contain a certain degree of poetical exaggeration, employed by the author to express his idea with the utmost clarity. Nevertheless, Mayakovsky's views of the revolutionary process were somewhat lop-sided.

But as Mayakovsky increasingly came abreast of the new social reality, his poetical notions of the Revolution became more profound and balanced. With time he came to accept the generally-shared views of many of the values (Nature, the cultural heritage of the past, history, etc.) which in the first post-revolutionary years were obviously down-graded in a number of his works, for polemical purposes.

Mayakovsky's creative activity in these years was extremely diverse. He was convinced that "the work of a poet of the Revolution was not confined to the writing of books". Accordingly, he turned to the theatre and cinema, which attracted him by their wide audience. So, he wrote more than a dozen film-scripts. Mayakovsky began to make regular contributions to the daily press, produced political posters which became an indispensable feature of the urban street scene in the first years of the Revolution.

An important part in strengthening Mayakovsky's ties with social reality, in improving the poet's style, was played by his work in ROSTA—the Russian Telegraph Agency. In the course of almost a year and a half he actively participated in the production of agit-posters on vital topics of the day, both as cartoonist and author of poetic captions to drawings. These posters, known as "Windows of ROSTA", were manufactured by hand and hung up in the streets for everyone to see and read. This work, as Mayakovsky himself recalled later, helped him acquire on-the-spot precision in the assessment of various facts of reality, to sift verbal superfluities from his poetic language.

Mayakovsky's work on the poem *Vladimir Ilyich Lenin* became a turning-point in his ideological and artistic evolution. The death in January 1924 of the leader of the October Revolution shook Mayakovsky to the very depths of his soul, and made the writing of the poem a vital necessity.

While working on the poem, in which he utilized extensive historical material, Mayakovsky came up against fundamental difficulties. In the poet's own words, he had to be very careful in order not "to reduce the poem to the level of mere political paraphrase". Fortunately, this did not happen. The revolutionary struggle of the masses for liberation is depicted *poetically*. Any scene taken at random in the poem is plastic, expressive, emotional to the utmost degree.

On the basis of extensive historical material, the poem shows the gigantic scope of Lenin's activity. Glimpsing back at the past—"two hundred years or so"—Mayakovsky, as it were, takes the reader through all stages of the revolutionary movement. He conveys the dramatic atmosphere of peasant riots, of the first manifestations of the working class. The reader gets an eye-witness view of the emergence of the Bolshevik Party, the October uprising, the battles against Whiteguard troops and the forces of intervention, the labour effort of the young Soviet Republic.

He is also taken through the pages of Lenin's biography.

In sculpting the image of V. I. Lenin, Mayakovsky, on the one hand, underlines his "usualness": he is just "like you and I, in every detail", "the earthliest of beings", "the most humane of all us humans". But at the same time Lenin, taking "in all the planet at a time, saw things out of reach for the common eye". In this characterization there is no contradiction: as a genuine leader of the working masses, Lenin could not but remain human, near and comprehensible to the people.

Although basically epic, the poem is permeated with elemental lyricism. Permeating the entire narrative, the lyric energy occasionally condenses, taking the form of meditations. In them, the poet formulates and examines his most heartfelt thoughts and emotions.

Mayakovsky had to listen to constant reproofs from quasi-esthetic critics. Stubbornly dismissing the poetic power of his verse, they branded it as mere publicism. Responding in the poem about Lenin to such attacks, Mayakovsky passionately defended the right of a poet to work for the setting up of militant political art:

Sure,
     "Capitalism" rings
                    not so very elegant,
"Nightingale"
               has a far more delicate sound.
Yet I'll go back to it
                 whenever relevant.
Let stanzas
          like fighting slogans resound!
I've never
          been lacking in topics—
                         you know it,
but now's
         no time
              for lovesick tattle.
All
    my thundering power of a poet
is yours,
         my class
                waging rightful battle!

All the lyric monologues are interconnected, having one source—the lyric hero of the poem. This time he has nothing to do with the rebel of the early poems; he is no isolated individual at odds with the world. The lyric hero of this poem has an important distinction: through him Mayakovsky speaks for himself and in the name of millions.

Vladimir Ilyich Lenin is a poem of enormous humanist significance. Its humanism, however, is not expressed in the lyric hero's dream about the future, as was the case with the pre-October poems. The poet derives his love for man, his faith in the triumph of justice, from the real life surrounding himself and his heroes. The poem *Vladimir Ilyich Lenin* testified to a deepening of Mayakovsky's historic vision, opening for him the way to a more comprehensive depiction of reality, leading him forward to new creative achievements.

The years 1924-1930 were a time when new facets became apparent in Mayakovsky's talent. He wrote hundreds of pieces, many of which won general acclaim: "Jubilee Poem", "To Sergei Esenin", "A Message to Proletarian Poets", "To Comrade Nette—Steamer and Man", "Verlaine and Cézanne", "Black and White", "Brooklyn Bridge", "Home", "To Our Young Generation", "A Letter from Paris to Comrade Kostrov on the Essence and Meaning of Love", "Talking with the Taxman about Poetry", "My Soviet Passport", "A Story of Kuznetskstroy and Its Builders", "Conversation with Comrade Lenin", the long poems *Fine!* and *Aloud and Straight*.

The poet made no distinction between minor and major subjects, writing about the heroic workers of Kursk who mined the first ore, about the new flat given to foundryman Kozyrev, the martyrdom of the diplomatic messenger Theodore Nette, about the way the worker Pavel Katushkin bought a radio receiver, the construction of the Kuznetsk steelworks, and the poetry of Ivan Molchanov. Yet nowhere does his verse lose its high emotional pitch or become petty, earthbound, for in all these facts and events the poet managed to discern and discover essentials of interest to the majority of the people, i. e., universally significant.

Mayakovsky's poetry took in all that was new in socialist reality, which emerged into being before his own eyes. His verse discloses the heroic features of the new epoch, shows how "the new comes boiling into life in people". With tremendous force his poems express the ideas of Soviet patriotism and internationalism, the fraternal unity between working people of different countries.

These new features in Mayakovsky's poetic vision of the world came out with particular clarity and vividness in his poem *Fine!* which he was fully entitled to call his "poetic programme". The poem was written in 1927, for the tenth anniversary of the Great October Socialist Revolution.

The country was preparing to meet its anniversary with due grandeur. The breath-taking momentum of the Soviet country's growth gave rise to optimism, mass labour enthusiasm. This atmosphere of general upsurge caught up Mayakovsky as well. The sensation of rapid renewal in all spheres of life, the awareness that the country was on the eve of a new mighty surge forward, moved Mayakovsky to write his new poem *Fine!,* which breathed the enthusiasm of socialist construction and innovation.

The poem *Fine!* depicts the immensely difficult yet glorious path covered by the Soviet State in the ten years of its existence. Recollecting these years, the poet comes to the conclusion that our sacrifices were not in vain: "Our Republic is building and growing", "gaining potency, mighty and fair". Mayakovsky formulates this impression in extraordinarily apt images: "country-stripling", "land of youth", "the spring of humanity".

In this glorification of the socialist revolution, of the heroic exploits of the Soviet people, in his ecstatic verses about the features of communism emerging from the everyday life of the millions, lies the main idea of the poem *Fine!* As Lunacharsky aptly said, "The poem is the October Revolution cast in bronze."

The image of the Soviet Motherland is built in the poem not only by epic means. An enormous part in portraying this image is played here by the lyric hero. Very often he appears as a real, live person, Vladimir Mayakovsky, some events of whose life are described in the poem. At the same time, this is also a generalized image. He is a happy witness of his country's liberation and coming of age, an active participant in great battles, one of those by whom this land was "won in battle and nursed back to life". That is why the feeling of oneness with the masses comes so naturally to him, why he speaks so freely in the name of millions: "Our waggons", "our firewood", "for us to grow", "all that we do".

The lyric hero identifies himself almost wholly with the people, but not quite. And yet it was Mayakovsky's intention to make the people's voice heard per se, as loudly as possible. What did he do to achieve this purpose?

The poem abounds in mass scenes directly depicting the people. But not the faceless mass of *150,000,000*. In the caleidoscope of figures and events we see soldiers demanding an end to the war. Kronstadt sailors, a worker "from the War Bureau", Red Guardsmen storming Winter Palace, a workman from the Putilov Works admonishing a young lad who pinched a watch, peasants setting fire to estates, communists loading firewood on a working Saturday, Red squadrons defeating the whiteguard General Mamontov. Here also we see real historical figures: Dzerzhinsky, Podvoisky, Antonov-Ovseyenko, Voikov who are all combined by the author into a single generalized image of the revolutionary people, incorporating the idea of the genuinely popular character of the proletarian revolution.

Mayakovsky's swift advance towards the heights of socialist art was accompanied in the late twenties by noticeable achievements in the field of satire. In the course of many years he had successfully contributed to many of the central newspapers, keeping especially close ties with *Komsomolskaya pravda*. Mayakovsky's work for the press enabled him to get acquainted with a stream of "negative" factual material, demonstrating the viability of carry-overs from the past incompatible with the ideals of the Revolution. Utilizing this material, Mayakovsky in his poetic cartoons portrays a whole gallery of satirical types: bureaucrats, philistines, drunkards, hooligans, gossips, toadies, bribe-takers, liars, demagogues, etc. Mayakovsky's attention as a satirist was constantly focussed on the international scene as well.

In the last eight years of his life Mayakovsky almost annually travelled abroad. He visited Germany, France, Mexico, Cuba, USA, Poland, Czechoslovakia. His travels were not holiday voyages: the poet closely scrutinized the life in foreign countries, paying tribute to the scientific and technological achievements he noticed. But the poet's eye also caught signs of social inequality, exploitation, racial discrimination, the meniality of the press.

Clearly aware of the complexity of socio-political struggles in the world, understanding that it would not be easy to surpass capitalist countries economically, the poet nevertheless firmly believed that this historic competition would be won by socialism.

Generally speaking, Mayakovsky's satire occupied an important place in his work at all stages of his career. Yet after the Revolution it underwent a radical change in its essence. If earlier it had been dominated by the idea of the total rejection of the old life system, complete destruction of the existing world order, following October, the very motifs of Mayakovsky's use of satire were changed. His use of this weapon was determined by his wish to help strengthen socialist relations. If before the Revolution "gigantic love" existed only as an antithesis of "gigantic hatred", now they prove interconnected: "gigantic hatred" becomes a derivative of "gigantic love". This, generally speaking, explains the appearance of new features in Mayakovsky's satire: historical optimism and a deeply ingrained, life-asserting spirit.

New features in his approach to the satirical theme appeared already in *Mystery-Bouffe*. The author subtitled his play "An heroic, epic and satirical portrayal of our epoch". The satirical aspect of *Mystery-Bouffe* is connected with the ridiculing of life's evil, which is brought out as absolutely definite "enemies of the Revolution" obstructing our movement ahead.

In the beginning of 1923, when the Soviet press launched a debate on the potentialities of satire in Soviet conditions, Mayakovsky published an article entitled "May One Become a Satirist?", and also wrote a preface to his collection *Mayakovsky Laughs, Mayakovsky Grins, Mayakovsky Sneers*. In these articles, besides calling on writers "to arm themselves with satirical skills", he puts forward the idea that satire cannot help bearing the imprint of its time, recording the voice of the epoch. With the years, developing this idea, the poet comes to the conclusion that "criticism should be correlated with the enthusiasm and pathos which we put into socialist construction".

This idea of Mayakovsky's is convincingly supported by his own experience as a satirist. In his poetry of the twenties, denunciation and derision are not aims in themselves. The poet's purpose is always immensely wider. To say that it includes the desire "to sing the days of the Revolution" is not enough, for his criticism itself proves derivative, following from this desire. Mayakovsky's satirical denunciation is a component part of his general mission, as he sees it himself: to assert the grandeur and beauty of the new world born in struggle with the old. As one of the students of Mayakovsky's work aptly put it, "his satire is lyricism driven to exasperation".

With the years, Mayakovsky increasingly resorted to a form of narrative in which the exposure of evil goes parallel with glorification of his time. By showing negative phenomena in confrontation with the progressive forces of our society, the poet resorts to highly expressive poetic hyperboles, at the same time strengthening the heroic element in his work. Especially demonstrative in this respect are Mayakovsky's plays *The Bedbug* and *The Bath-House*.

Mayakovsky's own remarks on the production of *The Bath-House*, prove beyond doubt that in writing this play he aimed at much more than the mere exposure of bureaucracy. Mayakovsky formulated the main idea of the play as follows: "struggle against narrow-mindedness, petty opportunism, bureaucracy, for heroism, for accelerated tempo, for socialist perspectives". Mockery of "sovbureaucrats" is the central theme of the play. But the author does not confine himself to mere criticism and exposure of bureaucracy. He regards this evil of contemporary life from the viewpoint of historic perspectives, against the background of the heroic efforts of the working masses.

The theme of future communist society, whose foundations are being laid by the heroic labour of builders of socialism, plays an exceptional part in resolving the main conflict of the comedy. In its fifth act there is a monologue by the Phosphorescent Woman, "a delegate from the year 2030", who arrives to establish contact between the present and future, to select "the best for transfer to the Communist age". "You cannot see," says she, "what a splendid job you are doing. It is easier for us to judge, because we know what has become part of our life. I was amazed to see your tiny apartments, that disappeared long ago and have been carefully restored in our museums. I looked at your huge constructions of earth and steel, that we still remember with gratitude as fine models of Communist building and life. And I gazed at obscure, begrimed youths, whose names are now inscribed on tablets of annulled gold. In my brief flight today I have seen and felt the power of your will, the thunder of your tempest, that so quickly grew into our happiness, into the joy of the whole planet."

These words give splendid expression to one of the main motifs of the play—its heroic pathos and projection into the future. This, of course, cannot be isolated from the other components of the plot, and, obviously, first and foremost, from the central theme—the exposure of bureaucracy. As the plot develops, the time machine carries off true labour heroes to "Communist Tomorrow", which in Phosphorescent Woman's words, "will take anyone who has at least one quality linking him with the commune collective", discarding the pillars of bureaucracy as refuse.

Obviously, it is in such works where the heroic element, intermingling with critical motifs, finds direct expression, i. e., in Mayakovsky's plays *The Bedbug* and *The Bath-House*, that the salient features of his satirical talent unfold in full and the stylistic traits of his satire become fully manifest.

For all the importance of Mayakovsky's work in the field of satire and satirical drama, deeply innovative in nature and contributing to the formation of the esthetic principles of Soviet satire as a whole, his main artistic achievements are nonetheless connected with his poetical work—his lyric poetry and major epic poems, the last of which, *Aloud and Straight*, is, virtually, a summary of his entire life and work.

At the very end of the twenties the country had entered a new stage of its development, beginning the fulfilment of the first five-year plan. The slogan "Time, Forward! ", which became the most popular slogan of the day, precisely conveys the spirit of that moment in the history of the Soviet Union.

The atmosphere of that period caught up Mayakovsky, too, which is reflected in a number of his works, in particular, "A Story of Kuznetskstroy and Its Builders" and his play *The Bath-House*. The poet intended to give voice to his new feeling of the time in a big poem about the five-year plan, the outlines for which, according to friends, were drawn in 1929.

In 1929 Mayakovsky marked two decades of his poetic work, which he dated from 1909, when he began to write poetry. He decided to celebrate this occasion with an exhibition under the headline "Twenty Years of Work", which would illustrate the main directions and stages of his activity. Preparations for the exhibition continued from December 1929 to January 1930. It was partly in connection with this exhibition that he struck upon the idea of an introduction to the big poem which he was then planning. Mayakovsky published this introduction as a separate piece in February 1930 under the heading *Aloud and Straight. First Prologue to a Poem of the Five-Year Plan*. Simultaneously he began working on the second, lyrical prologue, only several fragments of which were written and published under the heading "Unfinished". No evidence remains as to how he pictured the plot of the poem in its entirety.

Although it was subtitled *First Prologue...*, *Aloud and Straight* bears the features of a complete and independent piece of poetry. Mayakovsky's students lawfully regard it as a medium-sized complete poem in itself, charged with poetic passion and containing profound meditations on life, on the time, the essence and purpose of art, the poet's place in the revolutionary struggle.

In the poem *Aloud and Straight*, Mayakovsky sums up his creative work which he dedicated to the Revolution. It is a profession of faith, as it were, addressed to descendants and contemporaries, a close scrutiny of his progress through life: did he always go straight, or chose ways more easy, better-trodden? Did he take part in the battles of his time or did he try to evade them? Was he always sincere in his verse? Were there any false notes in what he wrote?

The main thing for him was that he could rest assured: his life and work had been inseparably bound with the Revolution, the struggle for the liberation of working people.

The enemy
of the colossus working class,
he's mine as well,
detested,
hated,
mortal.

Mayakovsky continuously rose to the defence of his primary poetic and esthetic principles. He had to assert his understanding of art in constant, sharp confrontation with his ideological and political adversaries, which is well felt in the polemic tone of the whole poem.

In a revolutionary epoch, art cannot be just a lot of "lyric out-pourings", interesting to the few. It should turn towards the crucial issues of life, should become as vital to the millions as bread and water. Mayakovsky's poetry was exactly such art, born, as it were, in the very heat of class battles.

Our dialectics
weren't derived
from Hegel's cunning.
Through battle din
it burst into our verse.

For a revolutionary poet, Mayakovsky urged, there is no division into great and petty themes, into high and low art. While doing his own poetic job, the poet simultaneously fulfilled other tasks demanded by the current moment: became an agitator, poster-drawer—one of the main producers of the "Windows of ROSTA".

For you of iron health
and steely muscle knots
a poet licked away
consumptive's clots
with the rough tongue
of posters that he made.

Apart from productions which became landmarks in the history of socialist poetry, a good deal of what he wrote was to serve immediate agitational ends. In *Aloud and Straight* he regards this work of his as essential for the cause of the revolution. But then, suddenly, the poet seems to burst out:

Me too
agitprop
makes sick as hell,
me too
writing love-songs
would suit as well...

Yet, Mayakovsky declares, "I, I'd trample, myself to quell, on the very throat of my verse."

Certain critics abroad, not understanding or intentionally distorting the essence of Mayakovsky's poetry, try to interpret these words in the sense that the poet violated his talent, that he suppressed his poetic feeling in subservience to politics, and so destroyed himself. But any unbiassed reader can clearly see that it was in poetry of great social import that Mayakovsky's talent gained fullest development, that his lyrical gift is universal in scope, encompassing political themes as well.

Of course, Mayakovsky's statement is not just a poetical exaggeration. It carries a share of drama. In the words of Nikolai Chernyshevsky, a nineteenth-century Russian critic and revolutionary democrat, "a creative individual is invariably compelled to give up some of his aspirations so as to ensure the fulfilment of others, higher and more vital". These words explain much in the destiny of Mayakovsky, who in the severe years of the Revolution, which demanded all of man's energies, to the point of self-sacrifice and privation, selected the hardest of possible paths.

The country was then in the throes of sharp struggle to assert the principles of the Revolution in all spheres of life. It was vital not only to build up an art of broadest artistic generalizations, that would be able to most fully reveal the meaning of revolutionary transformations. In those years a huge role was to belong, and actually did belong, to so-called agit-art, which in simple images, understandable to the masses, conveyed the ideas of social enlightenment.

By mobilizing the entire arsenal of his spiritual and creative powers, Mayakovsky managed to achieve both these objectives in his art. Fulfilling the functions of a "muck-cleaner and water-carter" of everyday revolutionary reality, he was at the same time able to create poems not merely connected with the demands of the moment but expressing the great truth of the revolutionary epoch, addressed "to the ages, to History, to the Universe".

With the passing of time, it becomes increasingly clear that Vladimir Mayakovsky was not only the greatest representative of revolutionary art, but one of the creators of socialist artistic culture in the very highest meaning of the word. The great poet's work gave powerful expression to the spiritual potentialities of the socialist revolution. It embodies many characteristics of the world outlook of a man whom the course of revolutionary transformations had put in the vanguard of historical progress. Mayakovsky's strong belief was that socialism offers the broadest scope for the development and perfection of the human individual, and was one of the first in Soviet poetry to express this soul-lifting capacity of the new society with enormous force.

A buoyant sense of the joy of life under socialism, profound belief in the victory of communist ideals—such was the main mental stimulus which moved Mayakovsky in his work. And this was his mainstay, from which nothing could swerve. Nothing, essentially, is altered in this respect by the poet's tragic departure from life.

A good deal has been written about Mayakovsky's suicide by both Soviet and foreign critics. Not all explanations of the causes of his death appear feasible. Some authors, ignoring the actual facts of literary life in those years, stubbornly refuse to see that the cause of the poet's tragic death was not his discord with reality or an inner creative crisis, but a whole number of circumstances combined. Among these we may mention the love-drama which Mayakovsky describes in his last letter, worsening relations with associates in LEF,* complicated drastically by the poet's entry into RAPP; his permanent persecution by esthetist critics, not lessening, but on the contrary, increasing with the years; the disease which tormented the poet for many months...

Characteristically, for many contemporaries Mayakovsky's personality was incompatible with the very notion of hysteria, pessimism, thoughts of death. This general feeling was well expressed at the funeral by Anatoly Lunacharsky:

"Mayakovsky was first and foremost a great chunk of hot, tense life. All the more so when he became a spokesman for the greatest social movement in history, when in the name of the millions he spoke to the millions about the millions' destinies. Mayakovsky, the herald of the Revolution, remains unvanquished. He stands before us in all his monumental integrity. Listen to the sound of his songs. Nowhere will you detect the least falsehood, the least doubt, the slightest vacillation. On the very eve of his death, "aloud and straight", he reaffirmed his loyalty to the great cause to which he gave his entire life and enormous talent."

The history of Soviet literature shows Mayakovsky to have exerted enormous influence on every generation of Soviet writers. It may even be said that his influence on Soviet literature has been greater and stronger than that of any other poet.

Mayakovsky's heritage has become an indispensable formative part of the present-day artistic and ideological atmosphere. The contemporary poetic world, we must note, is most multiform as regards attitudes to tradition. The work of a good number of various poets displays the impact of different poetic systems, traces of different poetic phenomena of the past. And yet Mayakovsky occupies a place apart among the factors influencing contemporary poetry.

The desire of Soviet poets to participate in solving the key issues of the time, to convey the most characteristic aspirations and emotions of contemporaries, are manifestations of their fidelity to the traditions of Mayakovsky. Continuity, referring to his heritage, implies not literal repetition of his experience, but poetic reproduction of the entire multiplaned life of developed socialist society in its most essential, typical manifestations. Today this is the main path of Soviet poetry, understandably, in its best productions.

It would be wrong, though, to speak of Mayakovsky's traditions only as applied to Soviet literature. Mayakovsky's works have been translated into foreign languages and his collections

*LEF—Left Front of Arts, futurist grouping founded and headed by Mayakovsky, who, however, outgrew it, finally joining RAPP—Russian Association of Proletarian Writers, forerunner of the USSR Writers' Union.—Ed.

published in more than thirty countries. Hundreds of books, thousands of articles have been written about the poet, about his life and work.

As a major ideological and esthetic phenomenon of the twentieth century, Mayakovsky has exerted and still exerts a benign influence on the work of many progressive and revolutionary men of arts. He was and remains a powerful creative stimulus for poets, playwrights, essayists, artists and musicians... The realization of the profound novelty of Mayakovsky's experience, the ensuing desire to express in one's own work (naturally, in accordance with one's own individuality) the new sensation of life born through contact with the verse of the remarkable Soviet poet, unites such different representatives of different literatures as Louis Aragon, Paul Eluard, Pablo Neruda, Bertholt Brecht, Johannes Becher, Julian Tuwim, Nazim Hikmet, and many other contemporary poets of Asia, Africa and America. In confirmation, we may also cite numerous statements by outstanding spokesmen of contemporary art and culture. So, Louis Aragon once acknowledged that his acquaintance with Mayakovsky changed his whole life. "Vladimir Mayakovsky," he recalled, "taught me one must appeal to the millions, to those who wish to remodel the world." A very precise assessment of Mayakovsky belongs to Johannes Becher: "His works celebrated the birth of a new man. The universal significance of Mayakovsky lies in that in his works he showed himself so brilliantly as a freely developing socialist personality."

Of course, art may follow various paths. Having given "all his resonant power of a poet" to the struggle for a better future for entire humanity, Mayakovsky advanced the development of Russian poetry, made a new step forward in the artistic development of mankind. In his poetry, he glorifies "the joy of life, the buoyancy of the most difficult march towards communism".

Alexander Ushakov

Translated by Dorian Rottenberg

I MYSELF

THEME

I am a poet. In that I am interesting. Of that I write. Of the rest—only if I have found the right words.1

MEMORY

Burlyuk said, "Mayakovsky has a memory like a road in Poltava—everyone leaves a galosh behind." But I don't memorize faces and dates. I only remember that in 1100 a people called the "Dorians" migrated somewhere. I don't remember the details, but it must have been very high-flown. To memorize "Written on the second day of May. Pavlovsk. The Fountains" is a very trivial manner. I therefore sail freely along in my own chronology.

WHAT MATTERS

I was born on 7 July 1894 (or '93; my mother's opinion and my father's service records were at variance). In any case, not earlier. Birthplace, the village of Bagdady, Kutaisskaya Gubernia. Georgia.2

MEMBERS OF THE FAMILY

Father: Vladimir Konstantinovich (forester in Bagdady), died in 1906.
Mother: Alexandra Alexeyevna.
Sisters:
a) Lyuda.
b) Olya.
There are no other Mayakovskys apparently.

1st RECOLLECTION

Painting concepts. Place unknown. Winter. Father has subscribed to the magazine *Rodina* (Homeland). *Rodina* has a humorous supplement. The cartoons are discussed and waited for. My father goes about singing his eternal *Allongs englong de lar per three.*3 *Rodina* arrives. I open it and immediately (cartoon) burst out laughing: "How funny! Uncle and auntie are kissing! " They laugh. Later, when the supplement arrived and was time to laugh properly it emerged that earlier they had only been laughing at me. Thus did our concepts of pictures and humour diverge.

2nd RECOLLECTION

Concepts poetic. Summer. Masses of people arrive. B. P. Glushkovsky, a tall, handsome student. Paints. Leather-bound notebook. Glossy paper. On the paper there is a tall man without any trousers on (or perhaps wearing tights) in front of a mirror. The man is called "Eugeneonegin". Boris is tall, and the man in the drawing is tall. All is clear. Boris must be "Eugeneonegin". This opinion lasts for three years.

3rd RECOLLECTION

Practical concepts. Night. Endless whispering of Papa and Mama behind the wall. About the piano. Can't sleep all night. One phrase nagging at me. In the morning, I rush into them: "Papa, what's payment by instalments?" The explanation pleases me greatly.

BAD HABITS

Summer. Striking number of guests. Name-days piling up. Father boasts of my memory. I'm made to learn verses by heart for all name-days. I remember, specially for Papa's name-day:

Once before a crowd
Of congeneric mountains...

"Congeneric" irritated me. I didn't know what it was and it had no desire to come my way in real life. I subsequently learned that all this was poesy, and I began quietly to hate it.

ROOTS OF ROMANTICISM

The first house, distinctly remembered. Two storeys. The upper was ours. The lower was a vintner's. Came carts full of grapes once a year. They were pressed. I ate. They drank. All this was in the grounds of a very ancient Georgian fortress near Bagdady. The fortress was squared off by a rampart. There were ramps for guns in the corners. The ramparts themselves had loopholes. Outside the ramparts there were ditches. After the ditches came forests and jackals. Beyond the forests there were mountains. I was growing up. Ran up the highest. The mountains descended to the north. In the north there was a gap. I dreamed that it was Russia. I felt incredibly drawn to go there.

THE UNCOMMON

About seven years old. Father began taking me on horseback tours of the forestry. A mountain pass. Night. Fog all round us. Couldn't even see father. A very narrow path. Father must have caught a briar with his sleeve. The branch lashed back and dug its thorns into my cheek. Yelping with pain, I pulled out the thorns. The mist and pain vanished at once. It was brighter than heaven in the fog dividing under our feet. That was electricity. Prince Nakashidze's rivet factory. After electricity, I completely lost interest in nature. For me, it was an imperfect thing.

STUDIES

I was taught by Mama and various girl cousins. Arithmetic seemed unreal. I had to count up apples and pears given away to little boys. They always gave them to me and I always gave them away without counting. There are all the fruits you could wish for in the Caucasus. But I enjoyed learning to read.

FIRST BOOK

Agafya the Poultry Girl, or something. If several such books had come my way at that time, I would have given up reading altogether. Fortunately, the second book was *Don Quixote*. Now that was a real one! I made a wooden sword and armour and smote the environment.

EXAM

We moved. From Bagdady to Kutaisi. Entrance exam for grammar school. I passed. I was asked about the anchor (on my sleeve). I knew well. But the clergy man asked what an *oko* is. I answered "Three pounds" (which is what it means in Georgian). The kindly examiners explained to me that *oko* means "eye" in ancient Church Slavonic. I nearly failed because of that. And so I immediately conceived a hatred of everything ancient, everything churchy and everything Slavonic. It may be that my futurism came from this, and my atheism, and my internationalism.

GRAMMAR SCHOOL

Preparatory, 1st and 2nd. I was the best pupil. Top marks for everything. I read Jules Verne. The fantastic in general. A man with a beard discovered that I had artistic talent. Taught me free of charge.

THE JAPANESE WAR

The number of newspapers and magazines at home was on the increase. *Russkiye vedomosti, Russkoye slovo, Russkoye bogatstvo* and others. I read them all. Was unaccountably nervous. Thrilled by picture postcards of battle cruisers. I enlarged and copied them. The word "proclamation" appeared. The proclamations were put up by Georgians. The Georgians were hanged by Cossacks. My comrades were Georgians. I began hating Cossacks.

ILLEGAL ACTIVITIES

My sister arrived from Moscow. In raptures. Secretly gave me long pieces of paper. I liked this: very risky. I remember them even now. The first went:

> *Come, comrade, awake; come, brother, awake.*
> *Make haste now and throw down your rifle.*

and something else, with the ending:

> *...or otherwise—*
> *to the Germans with son, and wife, and Mama...*

(meaning the tsar).

It was revolution. It was verse. Verse and the revolution somehow came together in my head.

Mind not on my studies. Started getting low marks. Was moved to the fourth form only because my head was bashed by a stone (in a fight by the Rion[4]) and they felt sorry for me at the re-examination. For me, the revolution began like this: in his joy, my comrade, Isidor, the priest's cook, jumped on to the stove barefoot—General Alikhanov had been assassinated.[5] The pacifier of Georgia. Meetings and demonstrations began. I went too. It was good. I saw it in terms of painting anarchists in black, Socialist-Revolutionaries in red, Social-Democrats in dark-blue and the federalists in other colours.

SOCIALISM

Speeches, newspapers. Out of it all, unfamiliar concepts and words. Little white books in the windows. *Burevestnik.*[6] About the same thing. I bought them all. Got up at six in the morning. Read voraciously. First, "Down with the Social-Democrats", second, "Chats on Economics".[7] I was impressed for the rest of my life by the socialists' ability to disentangle facts and systematize the world. *What Should We Read?*—by Rubakin, apparently. Read what was recommended. Didn't understand much of it. Asked questions. Was introduced to a Marxist circle. Ended up with the Erfurt Programme.[8] Middle. About the "lumpen-proletariat". I began considering myself a Social-Democrat: took my father's rifles to the social-democratic committee.

I liked Lassalle as a figure. It must have been because he wasn't bearded. Younger. Lassalle became confused in my mind with Demosthenes. I would go to the Rion and make speeches with pebbles in my mouth.

REACTION

In my opinion, it began as follows: in the panic (perhaps dispersal) during a demonstration in memory of Bauman,[9] I was struck (after falling) by a drum on the head. I took fright. I thought I myself had cracked.

1906

My father died. He pricked his finger when stitching up some papers. Blood poisoning. Have been unable to bear needles ever since. Our prosperity came to an end. After father's funeral, we had 3 rubles left. Instinctively, feverishly, we sold the tables and chairs. We moved to Moscow. Why? We didn't even have any acquaintances there.

THE ROAD

Best of all is Baku. Towers, cisterns, the best perfume—oil, and after that, the steppe. Desert, even.

MOSCOW

We stayed in Razumovskoye. The Plotnikov sisters, whom we knew. Arrived in Moscow by steamer in the morning. We rented a small flat on Bronnaya Street.

MOSCOW LIFE

Difficulties with food. The pension was 10 rubles a month. My two sisters and I were studying. Mama had to let rooms with dinner. Rubbishy rooms. Students lived poorly. Socialists. I remember the first Bolshevik I met in the flesh, Vasya Kandelaki.

PLEASANT

Was sent for paraffin. 5 rubles. They gave me 14 rubles 50 kopecks change in the colonial shop: 10 rubles clear profit. Was ashamed. Walked round the shop twice (have got the Erfurt Programme under my skin). I quietly asked the clerk which one had made the mistake, the boss or the salesman. The boss! Bought and ate four sugar buns. Had a boat trip round the Patriarchal Ponds with the rest of the money. Haven't been able to stand the sight of sugar buns ever since.

WORK

No money in the family. Had to do poker work and paint. I particularly remember the Easter eggs. Round, and they turn and squeak like doors. Sold the eggs to a handicrafts shop on Neglinnaya Street. 10 to 15 kopecks apiece. Since then I have had an infinite hatred for Bem glassware,[10] Russian pseudo-folk style art and hack-work.

GRAMMAR SCHOOL

Transferred to the 4th class of the No. 5 High School. Bottom marks, feebly variegated by next-to-bottom marks. *Anti-Dühring* under the desk.

READING

Rejected belles-lettres altogether. Philosophy. Hegel. Natural science. But mainly Marxism. No work of art carried me away more than Marx's "Preface".[11] Illegal literature was coming from the students' rooms. "The Tactics of Street Fighting" etc. I distinctly remember a dark-blue *Two Tactics* by Lenin.[12] I liked the way all the margins of the book had been cut off. For smuggling purposes. The aesthetics of the maximum economy.

THE FIRST SEMI-POEM

No. 3 Secondary School was putting out the illegal magazine *Poryv* (Impetus). I was offended. Others were writing, so why couldn't I? I started creating. The result was incredibly revolutionary and equally ugly. Like today's Kirillov. I can't remember a single line. I wrote a second poem. The result was too sweetly lyrical for words. Considering such a state of the heart to be incompatible with my "socialist dignity", I scrapped the whole thing.

THE PARTY

1908. Joined the Russian Social-Democratic Workers' Party (Bolsheviks). Took an exam[13] in the trade and industrial sub-district. Passed. Propagandist. Went to the bakers, then to the cobblers and finally to the printing-press workers. Was elected to the Moscow Committee at an all-city conference. Lomov, Povolzhets, Smidovich and others were there. Was named "Comrade Konstantin". I didn't have to work for them, however—was arrested.

ARREST

On 29 March 1908, blundered into an ambush in Gruziny. Our illegal press. Ate a notepad. With addresses and in a cover. Presnya Police Station. Security. Sushchovskaya Police Station. Investigator Voltanovsky (evidently fancied himself as a crafty one) made me write to dictation: I was charged with writing proclamations. Wildly muddled up the dictation. Wrote: "Socialdemocritical". I may have got away with it. I was discharged on probation. While in the station, read *Sanin*[14] with bewilderment. The book was available at every police station for some reason. Evidently soul-saving.

I was released. About a year's Party work. And a brief spell inside once more.[15] They took my revolver. Makhmudbekov, who had been a friend of my father, was then assistant to the chief of the Crosses[16] and was arrested by chance in an ambush at my place, testified that the revolver was his; I was released.

THIRD ARREST

Some people living at our place (Koridze, cover-name Morchadze, Gerkulaitis and others) were digging a tunnel under the Taganka.[17] To release the women prisoners. They managed to stage a getaway from Novinskaya Prison. I was picked up. Didn't want to go to gaol. Made a scene. Was transferred from station to station—Basmannaya, Meshchanskaya, Myasnitskaya, etc., and, finally, to Butyrki,[18] Solitary Cell No. 103.

11 BUTYRSKY MONTHS

A most important time for me. After three years of theory and practice, I plunged into belles-lettres.

Read all the latest. The symbolists, Bely and Balmont. The formal novelty intrigued me. But it was alien. Themes and images not from my own life. I tried writing as well as they, but about something else. It turned out that it was impossible to write *about something else too.* It came out stilted and maudlin. Something like:

> *In purple and gold the forests were dressed*
> *The church domes were bright in the sun's dancing rays.*
> *I waited: in months were the days being lost,*
> *Hundreds of wearisome days.*

I filled the whole notebook with this sort of stuff. My thanks to the supervisors—they took it off me when I left. And to think that I might have published it!

After reading through my contemporaries I swooped on the

classics. Byron, Shakespeare, Tolstoy. The last book was *Anna Karenina*. Didn't finish it. Was called out at night to go across the town with my things. I still don't know how it ended with the Karenins.

I was discharged. I had to go (as decreed by the security forces) for three years to Turukhansk. Makhmudbekov interceded for me with Kurlov.[19]

During my spell inside, they sentenced me on the first charge[20]—guilty, but too young. I was to be handed over for police supervision and on the responsibility of parents.

A SO-CALLED DILEMMA

I came out in a state of excitement. Those I had read were the so-called great ones. But it shouldn't be hard to write better than them. Even now I had the right attitude to the world. All I needed was experience in art. Where I was to get it? I was untrained. I must have proper training. But I had even been kicked out of grammar school, and from the Stroganovsky.[21] If I stayed in the Party, I would have to go underground. Underground, it seemed to me, I wouldn't learn anything. I would be faced with the prospect of writing leaflets all my life, of expounding ideas taken from the correct books, but not thought up by me. If they shook out of me what I had read, what would be left? The Marxist method. But hadn't that weapon fallen into the hands of a child? It was easy to use it if you only had to do with the ideas of your own people. But what about clashes with enemies? I couldn't, after all, write better than Bely. He was cheerful about what mattered to him—"I flung a pineapple into the sky"—and I was whining about what mattered to me—"Hundreds of wearisome days". It was all right for the other Party members. They had been to university too. (As for higher school—I did not yet know what that was—I respected it at that time!)

What could I put up in opposition to the old word aesthetics that had descended on me? Didn't the revolution demand serious schooling? I looked in on Medvedev, at that time still my Party comrade, and said I wanted to produce a Socialist art. Seryozha laughed for a long time.

I nevertheless thought that he had underestimated my guts.

I gave up Party work and sat down to my studies.

BEGINNINGS OF MASTERY

I thought I couldn't write verse. Pitiful attempts. Took to painting. Studied under Zhukovsky. Painted dinky silver tea-sets with young ladies. After a year, I realized I was on the wrong track. Went to Kelin. A realist. A good draughtsman. Best teacher. Tough. Changeable.

Needed—skill, Holbein. Could not bear anything pretty-pretty.

A poet I respected was Sasha Chyorny. I was delighted by his anti-aestheticism.

THE LAST COLLEGE

Sat on my "head" for a year.[22] Entered the School of Painting, Sculpture and Architecture. The only place where you were accepted without a testimonial of reliability. Worked well.

I was amazed: imitators were encouraged, independents were hounded out. Larionov, Mashkov.[23] Out of revolutionary instinct, stood up for the ones being hounded out.

DAVID BURLYUK

Burlyuk appeared in the school. Brazen look. Lorgnette. Frock coat. Sang as he walked. I started teasing him. We nearly came to blows.

IN THE SMOKING-ROOM

A noble gathering. Concert. Rachmaninov. *Isle of the Dead.*[24] Fled the insufferable melodic tedium. So did Burlyuk a minute later. We roared with laughter at one another. Went out for a stroll together.

A MOST MEMORABLE NIGHT

Conversation. We went from the tedium of Rachmaninov to the tedium of college, and from the tedium of college to the whole tedium of classicism. David had the wrath of the master overtaking his contemporaries, I had the message of the socialist who knew that the collapse of the old world was inevitable. Russian futurism was born.[25]

THE NEXT NIGHT

Wrote a poem in the afternoon. Bits of one, to be more exact. Bad ones. Never published anywhere. Night. Sretensky Boulevard. I read the lines to Burlyuk. I added that they were by a friend of mine. David stopped. Looked me up and down. Barked, "But you wrote that yourself! Why, you're a poetic genius! " I was thrilled by the use of so grand and undeserved an epithet. I plunged wholly into verse. That evening, quite unexpectedly, I became a poet.

AND SO EVERY DAY

I had to write. I wrote my first (first professional published piece), "The white and the crimson..."[26] and others.

THE WONDERFUL BURLYUK

I think of David with undying love. A wonderful friend. My real teacher. Burlyuk made a poet of me. He read the French and the Germans to me. Pushed books at me. Walked and talked without end. Never let me out of his sight. Gave me 50 kopecks a day. So that I could write without starving.

For Christmas, took me to his place at Novaya Mayachka.[27] Brought "Harbour"[28] and something else.

A SLAP IN THE FACE

We returned from Mayachka. If with indistinct views, at least with refined temperaments. Khlebnikov was in Moscow. For me, his quiet genius was completely eclipsed at that time by the ebullient Burlyuk. Here, too, was Kruchenykh, the futurist Jesuit of the word.

After several nights, the lyric poets gave birth to a joint manifesto.[29] David put it together and copied it out; together we gave it a name and so brought out *A Slap in the Face of the Public Taste.*

THINGS START MOVING

Exhibitions of "The Jack of Diamonds". Disputes. My impassioned speeches and David's. The newspapers begin to be full of futurism. The tone is not very polite. For example, I am called a "son-of-a-bitch", no more, no less.

THE YELLOW BLOUSE

I never had any suits. There were two blouses of ghastly appearance. The tried and tested means was to add a tie for effect. No money. Took a piece of yellow ribbon from my sister. Tied it round my neck. Sensation. This meant that the most noticeable and beautiful thing about a man is his tie. Clearly, increase the magnitude of the tie and you increase the magnitude of the sensation. And since the dimensions of ties are limited, I resorted to ingenuity: I made a tie shirt and a shirt tie.

Impression irresistible.

NEEDLESS TO SAY

The General Staff of art bristled. Prince Lvov. Director of the college. Demanded that we stop the criticism and agitation. We refused.

The council of "artists" expelled us from college.

THE MERRY YEAR

We toured Russia. Recitals. Lectures. The provincial governors went on the alert. In Nikolayev they suggested that we should not mention the high-ups or Pushkin. The police often burst in on us in mid-lecture. Vasya Kamensky joined the gang. The oldest futurist.

For me these were years of formal work, gradual mastery of the word.

We were turned down by the publishers. The capitalist nose scented the dynamiters in us. They wouldn't buy a single line from me.

On returning to Moscow, I lived mainly on the boulevards.

This period was crowned with the tragedy, *Vladimir Mayakovsky.* Put on in Petersburg. Luna Park. They gave it the razz.

I feel my own skill. I can master a theme. Thoroughly. I set myself the problem of the theme. A revolutionary one. I mull over *Cloud in Pants*.

WAR

Was very excited. At first took it only from the decorative, jingoistic angle. Posters to order and, of course, about the war. Then a poem, "War's Declared".

AUGUST

The first battle. The horror of war in all its stature. War is disgusting. The rear is even more disgusting. To talk about war, one must see it. Went to sign on as a volunteer. They turned me down. No reliability.

And Colonel Model had one good idea.

WINTER

Revulsion and hatred for war. "Ah, close, close the eyes of the papers"[30] and other poems.

Interest in art entirely lost.

MAY

Won 65 rubles. Left for Finland. Kuokkala.

KUOKKALA

Seven-friend system (Crop-rotation). Have established seven dining acquaintances.[31] On Sunday, I "eat" Chukovsky; on Monday, Yevreinov etc. On Thursday it was worse—I ate Repin's herbs.[32] For a seven-foot-tall futurist, this was no joke.

I spend the evening wandering along the beach. I write *Cloud*.

Awareness of the approaching revolution becomes stronger.

Went to Mustumyaki. M. Gorky. Read him part of *Cloud*. The deeply moved Gorky wept all over my waistcoat. I was almost proud. It soon emerged that Gorky sobs on every poetic waistcoat.

I keep the waistcoat as a memento nevertheless. I might let it go to someone for a provincial museum.

THE NEW SATIRIKON

The 65 rubles went easily and painlessly. "In a discussion what to eat", began writing for *The New Satirikon*.[33]

A MOST JOYFUL DATE

July 1915. Met L. Yu. and O. M. Brik.

CALL-UP

They've called me up.[34] I don't want to go to the front.

Pretended to be a draughtsman. At night I learn to draw cars under a certain engineer. Even worse with printing. Soldiers are forbidden to publish. Only Brik is delightful. Buys all my verse at

50 kopecks a line. Prints "The Backbone Flute" and *Cloud*. The cloud came out feathery. The censor blew on it. Six pages of dotted lines.

Since then, a hatred for dotted lines. And commas too.

SOLDIERING

A ghastly time. I draw (faking it somehow) portraits of the officers. *War and Peace* going round in my head, and *Man* in my heart.

1916

War and Peace completed. A little later, *Man*. I publish bits in *Letopis* (Chronicle). Brazenly do not show up in the barracks.

26 FEBRUARY 1917

Went with the cars to the Duma. Slipped into Rodzyanko's office. Looked over Milyukov. He said nothing. But for some reason it seems to me that he hiccoughs when he speaks. Got fed up with them after an hour. Went away. Took command of the Car School for several days. It's Guchkovizing.[35] Old officers pacing about the Duma in the old way. It's clear to me that the Socialists must inevitably come after this. Bolsheviks. During the first days of the revolution, I write *Revolution (A Poet's Chronicle)*. I read lectures—"The Bolsheviks of Art".

AUGUST

Russia is gradually de-Kerenskifying itself. They've lost respect. I leave *Novaya Zhizn*.[36] I mull over *Mystery Bouffe*.

OCTOBER

To accept or not accept? There was no such question for me (or for other Moscow futurists). My Revolution. Went to the Smolny Institute. Worked. Everything that came my way. They are beginning to hold sessions.

JANUARY

Went to Moscow. Made speeches. At night, in the *Poets' Café*, in Nastasinsky. The revolutionary grandmother of today's café-poetic salons.

I write film scenarios. Play parts myself. Do posters for the cinema. June. Petersburg again.

1918

The RSFSR has no time for art. But I have time for just that. Dropped in on Kshesinskaya at Proletkult.[37]

Why am I not in the Party? The communists worked at the fronts. In art and education they are conciliators, for the time being. They should send me to catch fish in Astrakhan.

25 OCTOBER 1918

Finished *Mystery*. Read it. Much talking. Produced by Meyerhold with K. Malevich. They bellowed around terribly. Especially the Communist intelligentsia. Andreyeva[38] did everything possible. To interfere. They put it on three times, then tore it to pieces. And the *Macbeths* started.

1919

I tour with *Mystery* and other pieces by me and by comrades around factories. Enthusiastic reception. They are organizing a *komfut* in the Vyborg district, we publish *Iskusstvo kommuny*.[39] The Academies are cracking. In spring I move to Moscow.

Head full of *150,000,000*. Have started agitation work for ROSTA.[40]

1920

Have finished *150,000,000*. Publishing it anonymously. I wanted everyone to be able to continue and improve it. No one did so, but they all knew my name. Never mind. Am publishing it here with my name.

Days and nights at ROSTA.[41] All kinds of Denikins advancing. I write and draw. Have done about three thousand posters and about six thousand captions.

1921

I force my way through all the red tape, hatreds, office routine and stupidities and put on a second version of *Mystery*. It's being performed in RSFSR Theatre No. 1, produced by Meyerhold with artists Lavinsky, Krakovsky and Kiselyov, and in the circus in German for the III Congress of the Comintern. It's being put on by Granovsky with Altman and Ravdel. It's had about a hundred performances.

Have started writing for *Izvestia*.

1922

Am organizing a Moscow Futurists' Association publishing house, am rallying the futurists and forming a commune. Aseyev, Tretyakov and other comrades-in-arms have arrived from the Far East. Have begun writing down *The Fifth International*, on which I've been working for over two years. Utopia. Art in 500 years' time will be shown.

1923

We are organizing LEF.[42] LEF covers a big social theme with all the tools of futurism. This definition does not, of course, exhaust the problem—I am referring those interested to our numbers. Closely welded together—Brik, Aseyev, Kushner, Arvatov, Tretyakov, Rodchenko and Lavinsky.

Have written *It*. On personal motives about life in general. Have been mulling over a poem, *Lenin*. One of the slogans, one of the big gains of LEF has been constructivism, the de-aestheticization of the production arts. Poetic application: the *agitka* and the administrative *agitka*, or advertisement. In spite of poetic catcalls, I regard "Nowhere except in Mosselprom" as poetry of the very highest quality.

"Monument to the workers of Kursk". A great many lectures round the USSR about LEF, "Jubilee Poem" to Pushkin. And verse of that kind—a cycle. Travel: Tiflis, Yalta—Sevastopol. "Tamara and the Demon" etc. Finished the poem *Lenin*. Read it at many workers' gatherings. I've been very much afraid of that poem, since it would have been easy to descend to the level of a simple political tale. The reaction of the working class audience delighted me and strengthened my confidence in the poem's topicality. I travel abroad a great deal. European technology, industrialism, attempt to combine them with the still stuck-in-the-mud former Russia—the eternal ideal of the LEF futurist.

In spite of discouraging edition data about the magazine, LEF is expanding its work.

We know those "data"—simply the usual office-routine negligence towards certain magazines on the part of the big, callous machinery of the State Publishing House.

1925

Wrote an agitpoem, "The Flying Proletariat" and a collection of agitverse, *Proceed Across the Skies Yourself.*

I'm going round the world. The beginning of this trip—the last long poem (composed of several short ones) on the theme of Paris. I want, and I am going, to transfer from verse to prose. This year I must finish my first novel.

"Around" didn't come out. First, I was robbed in Paris; secondly, after half a year's travelling, I shot like a bullet into the USSR. I didn't even go to San Francisco (they wanted me to read a lecture there). Travelled all over Mexico, the USA and bits of France and Spain. Result—books: publicistic prose: *My Discovery of America*, and verse: "Spain", "Atlantic Ocean", "Havana", "Mexico" and "America".

I finished the novel in my mind but did not commit it to paper, because while I was finishing it, I was acquiring a hatred for what I had conceived and began demanding of myself that it should be based on names and facts. By the way, this also goes for 1926 and 1927.

1926

In my work, I am consciously changing myself into a newspaperman. Feuilleton, slogan. Poets burble away, yet they can't do newspaper stuff themselves, but are published more in the irresponsible supplements. I find their lyrical rubbish funny to look at, since it's easy to do this sort of thing, but it's of no interest to anyone except to one's spouse.

I write for *Izvestia, Trud, Rabochaya Moskva, Zarya vostoka, Bakinsky rabochy* and others.

Second job—I am continuing the interrupted tradition of the troubadours and minstrels. I tour the cities and recite: Novocherkassk, Vinnitsa, Kharkov, Paris, Rostov, Tiflis, Berlin, Kazan,

Sverdlovsk, Tula, Prague, Leningrad, Moscow, Voronezh, Yalta, Eupatoria, Vyatka, Ufa etc, etc, etc.

1927

I am reviving (there was an attempt to "curtail" it) LEF, now "New".[43] The basic position: against fabrication, aestheticization and psychologizing by artistic means of art; in favour of agitation, qualified journalism and news reports. The basic work is in *Komsomolskaya pravda* and I am putting in work on *Fine!* out of school hours.

I consider *Fine!* a programme piece. As *Cloud in Pants* was for that period. Must cut down abstract poetic techniques (hyperboles, the vignette) and invent techniques for processing news reports and agitation material.

Ironic note in describing trifles that can nevertheless also be a first step into the future ("cheese—not a spot. Lamps strung about; "Prices cut! "), introduction, for re-hashing plans, facts of various historical calibre, legitimate only in the order of personal associations ("Conversation with Blok", "A Quiet Jew, Pavel Ilyich Lavut, was telling me").

I shall be developing what I have mapped out.

Furthermore, scenarios and children's books written.

Furthermore, continued playing the minstrel. Collected about 20,000 notes from audiences; am thinking about a book, *The Universal Answer* (for the note-writers). I know what the reading masses are thinking about.

1928

I am writing a poem, *Bad*.[44] A play[45] and my literary biography. Many have said, "Your autobiography is not very serious". True. I have not yet become academized and am not used to coddling myself; and in any case my job only interests me if it's fun. The rise and fall of many literatures, the symbolists, realists etc., our struggle with them—all this, which is taking place before my eyes, is part of our very serious history. It demands to be written about. And I shall write.

(1922. 1928)

Translated by Alex Miller

POETRY

NIGHT*

Translated by
Dorian Rottenberg

The white and the crimson discarded and crumpled,
gold ducats by handfuls were flung on the green;
then into the black palms of windows assembled
came cards, burning yellow, from dealers unseen.

For boulevards and squares there was nothing bizarre in
the sight of the buildings in togas of blue.
Before that with bracelets of yellow, like scar-rings,
the street-lamps had wedded men's running feet too.

The crowd—a big tabby-cat, brindled and nimble,
swam, curving and swerving, by doorways lured in;
each tingled to nibble if only a thimble
from the great lump of laughter—a chuckle, a grin.

I, feeling the pull of an evening-gown soft-pawed,
shot smiles through their eyes; filling people with fright
by banging on tin, burly Blackamoors guffawed,
while parrot-wings over their foreheads shone bright.

(1912)

MORNING

Translated by
Dorian Rottenberg

The sullen rain
cast a glance
askance.
Beyond the still
clear grille—
the iron reasoning of wires strung overhead—
a featherbed.
And on it
rested lightly
the legs of rising stars.
But as
the streetlamps-tsars
in crowns of gas

began to die,
they made more painful for the eye
the petty wars
of the bouquet of boulevard whores.
And horrid,
the lurid
pecking laughter
that jokes leave after
arose
from the yellow roses'
poisoned rows
in a zig-zag.
But at the back
of all the wracking horror
and the squalor
the eye rejoiced, at last;
the slave of crosses
sufferingly-placidly-indifferent,
the coffins
of the brothels
full of riff-raff
were flung into one flaming vase by the
dawning East.

(1912)

FROM STREET TO STREET*

*Translated by
Dorian Rottenberg*

Street-
spaces.
The faces
of days,
great danes,
grow tougher.
Over
the iron horses
from the windows of running houses
leap the first cubic blocks.
Swan-necked belfries,
 bend in your cable-wire snares!
In the sky the giraffe-sketch prepares
to mottle its rusty locks.
Motley like trout
is the son
of the patternless ploughland.
A conjuror,
hidden behind the clocks
on a tower

pulls rails from the mouth of a tram-car.
We're conquered!
Lifts.
Baths.
Showers.
The bra of the soul's undone.
Hands scorch the body,
whether you shout
"I don't want to! "
or not.
Hard
is suffering's
knot.
A prickly wind
from the chimneys
tears shreds of fur, grey, smoky.
A bald-pated street-lamp,
blatant,
lascivious,
pulls off the street's black stocking.

(1913)

WHAT ABOUT YOU?

Translated by
Dorian Rottenberg

I splashed some colours from a tumbler
and smeared the drab world with emotion.
I charted on a dish of jelly
the jutting cheekbones of the ocean.
Upon the scales of a tin salmon
I read the calls of lips yet mute.
And you,
        could you have played a nocturne
with just a drainpipe for a flute?

(1913)

I*

1

Translated by
Dorian Rottenberg

*English translation
©
Raduga Publishers 1985

Along the highway
of my soul,
all banged
and battered,
the steps of madmen

weave hard phrases patterns.
Where towns are hanged—
where in a cloud's grey noose
freeze
towers'
crooked necks,
once prim and glossy,
I go alone
to mourn
policemen
crucified
by crossings.

(1913)

2

SEVERAL WORDS ABOUT MY WIFE

Along a far-off beach on seas unknown
passes the moon—
my wife.
My mistress ginger-haired.
Behind the carriage
vociferously stream the constellations' speckled bands.
She's given
by a car-garage
in marriage,
she kisses through newspaper-stands,
her gown-train's Milky Way a blinking page
has decked in tinsel bangles with deft hands.
And I?
Didn't you bring me, scorched, upon your eyebrows' yoke
buckets of water
from the ice-cold wells of your eyes?
Didn't you hang in silky lakes in front of me,
like amber violins, your singing thighs?
Into these arid areas, where roofs vent anger
one couldn't cast a spangle-baited thong.
In boulevards I drown, in quicksand languor,
I sink away.
Look, it is she—
your daughter—
my pattern-stockinged song
near each café!

(1913)

50   SEVERAL WORDS ABOUT MY MOTHER

I have a mother upon cornflower wallpaper.
While I myself go strutting like a garish peacock,
tormenting touzled daisies, measured by my stride.
To start to play on rusty hoboes, comes the evening;
I go up to the window-sill,
believing
that once again I'll see a cloud
saddle a housetop
for a ride.
And there, where Mother's ill,
the rustling of men run by
from bed to corner, where blank emptiness lurks.
My mother knows—
it's bales of crazy thoughts that vie
in climbing from behind the roofs of Shustov's works.[46]
And when my brow crowned by a felt top hat
a fading window-frame with blood will smother,
I'll say,
my bass-voice parting the wind's wail:
"Mother,
if I start pitying the flower-bowl
of your pain
bowled
over by the pin-heels
of cloud-dancers,
who will caress the arms of gold
flung up by sign-boards on shopwindows at Avanzo's?[47]

(1913)

4

SEVERAL WORDS ABOUT MYSELF

I like to watch how little children die.[48]
Have you, too, seen the foggy wave of laughter's tide
behind the trunk of gloom?
And I,
in the streets' reading-room
have leafed so often through the coffin's volume!
Midnight
with rain-soaked fingers felt
me and the all-too-often beaten fence,
and, while the raindrops its bald dome would pelt,
the mad cathedral did its dance.
I see Christ run out of his gilded icon,
his wind-blown garment-hem
kissed weepingly by slush.

I shriek at brick,
my poniard-words in desperation striking
the heavens' puffy flesh:
"O Sun!
My Father!
You, at least, have pity, stop this torture!
It is my blood you shed that pours upon the road.
It is my soul
in the shreds of a cloud just butchered
hangs in the burnt-out sky
upon the belfry-cross in red rust clothed!
Time!
You, at least, O limping icon-painter,
come, daub my face
on this freak century's icon-stand!
I'm lonely as the only eye remaining
upon the face of one about to join the blind! "

(1913)

GREAT BIG HELL OF A CITY

*Translated by
Dorian Rottenberg*

Windows split the city's great hell
into tiny hellets-vamps with lamps.
The cars, red devils, exploded their yells
right in your ear, rearing on their rumps.

And there, under the sign-board with herrings from Kerch
an old man, knocked down, stooping to search
for his specs, sobbed aloud when a tram with a lurch
whipped out its eyeballs in the twilight splurge.

In the gaps between skyscrapers, full of blazing ore,
where the steel of trains came clattering by,
an aeroplane fell with a final roar
into the fluid oozing from the sun's hurt eye.

Only then, crumpling the blanket of lights,
Night loved itself out, lewd and drunk,
and beyond the street-suns, the sorriest of sights,
sank the flabby moon, unwanted old junk.

(1913)

*Translated by
Dorian Rottenberg*

HOW D'YE LIKE THIS?*

In an hour from here into the spotless alley
man by man, your sagging fat will flow.
And I've just opened for you so many verse-caskets, whose value
I, squanderer, spendthrift of words, only know.

Now you there, Mister, your whiskers still carry the cabbage
of soup which somewhere, somehow you didn't completely eat;
now you there, Madame, with ceruse concealing time's ravage,
like an oyster from the shell of things you peep!

All of you onto the butterfly heart of the poet
will clamber, with and without galoshes, to browze.
The crowd will start pushing and shoving, bestial growing,
bristling with tootsies, a myriad-headed louse.

And yet if I, rude Hunn out of Asia's spaces,
won't want to grimace before your herds—
I'll burst out laughing, and spit,
yes, spit in your faces,
I, squanderer, spendthrift of priceless words.

(1913)

LISTEN!

*Translated by
Dorian Rottenberg*

Now, listen!
Surely, if the stars are lit
there's somebody who longs for them,
somebody who wants them to shine a bit,
somebody who calls it, that wee speck
          of spittle, a gem?
And overridden
by blizzards of midday dust,
tears in to God,
afraid that it's too late,
and sobbing,
kisses the sinewy hand outthrust,
swears
that he can't, simply can't bear a starless
          fate:
There must be a star, there must!
...Then goes about anxious,
though tranquil seeming,
whispering to somebody,
"You're better?
Not afraid?

*English translation
©
Raduga Publishers 1985

All right?"
Now listen,
it must be for somebody stars are set gleaming,
somebody who longs
for one star at least
over the rooftops to come alight?

(1914)

AND YET...*

Translated by
Dorian Rottenberg

The street's caved in like a nose after syphilis.
The river's all lechery, drooling, obscene.
Discarding underwear to the last leaf, lascivious,
the gardens sprawl in a mid-June scene.

I come on the townsquare,
a burnt-out district
cramming on my head like a ginger wig.
Folks feel scared—from my mouth like biscuit
wriggle the feet of a half-chewed shriek.

Yet I won't be condemned, no, I won't be booed at.
Like a prophet's, my path with flowers they'll spread.
All these, with their caved-in noses know it:
I'm your poet, alive or dead.

Like a wineshop, I fear your doomsday judgement.
Me alone through the town's conflagration
bearing like a deity, whores will go trudging
to show to God in their justification.

God'll burst out sobbing over my booklet—
not words but shudders stuck together in lumps,
and he'll rush about heaven with my verse under his armpit
and read it, gasping, to his friends and chums.

(1914)

WAR'S DECLARED*

Translated by
Dorian Rottenberg

*English translation
©
Raduga Publishers 1985

"Evening papers! Evening papers! Evening papers!
Italy! Germany! Austria! " they scream.
And on the square, in its gloomy black drapery
crimson blood poured down in a stream.

The coffee-house smashed up its face, noisy,
blood-shot with bestial yells:
"With blood the frolics of the Rhine let's poison!
Blast the marble of Rome with shells! "

From the heavens shredded by bayonet stings,
like flour from a sieve, the star-tears strained,
and pity, squashed under boot-heels, poor thing,
screamed "Let me go! " again and again.

Bronze generals from their pedestals roared:
"Unshackle us, and we'll ride in a drove! "
Cavalry's farewell kisses were heard,
towards killer-victory infantry strove.

To the lumbering city in a monstrous nightmare
the guffawing bass of cannon seemed to crash.
In the West, crimson snow fell earthward, frightening
in juicy slivers of human flesh.

Company after company swells on the square,
veins swell up on its forehead in anger:
"Wait, we'll wipe our sabres yet there
on courtesans' silk in the boulevards of Vienna! "

Newsboys went hoarse: "Buy the evening papers! "
"Italy! Germany! Austria! " they screamed.
And out of the night in its gloomy black drapery
Crimson blood poured and poured in a stream.

20 July 1914

THE VIOLIN—A LITTLE BIT NERVOUS*

*Translated by
Dorian Rottenberg*

The violin got all worked up, imploring,
then suddenly burst into sobs,
so child-like
that the drum couldn't stand it:
"All right, all right, all right! "
But then he got tired, couldn't wait till the violin ended,
slipped out on the burning Kuznetsky
and took flight.
The orchestra looked on, chilly,
while the violin wept itself out
without reason
or rhyme,
and only somewhere,
a cymbal, silly,

*English translation
©
Progress Publishers 1980
©
Raduga Publishers 1985

kept clashing:
"What is it,
what's all the racket about?"
And when the helicon,
brass-faced, sweaty,
hollered:
"Crazy!
Cry-baby!
Be still! "
I staggered,
on to my feet getting,
and lumbered
over the horror-struck music stands,
yelling
"Good God! "
why, I myself couldn't tell;
then dashed, my arms round the wooden neck to fling:
"You know what, violin,
we're awfully alike;
I too
always yell,
but can't prove a thing! "
The musicians commented,
contemptuously smiling:
"Look at him—
come to his wooden bride—
tee-hee! "
But I didn't care—
I'm a good guy—
"You know what, violin,
let's live together,
eh?"

(1914)

YOU!

Translated by
Dorian Rottenberg

You, wallowing through orgy after orgy,
owning a bathroom and warm, snug toilet!
How dare you read about awards of St. George
from newspaper columns with your blinkers oily?!

Do you realize, multitudinous nonentities
thinking how better to fill your gob,
that perhaps just now Petrov the lieutenant
had both his legs ripped off by a bomb?

Imagine if he, brought along for slaughter,
suddenly saw, with his blood out-draining,
you, with your mouths still dribbling soda-water
and vodka, lasciviously crooning Severyanin! [49]

To give up my life for the likes of you,
lovers of woman-flesh, dinners and cars?
I'd rather go and serve pineapple juice
to the whores in Moscow's bars.

(1915)

THE WAY I BECAME A DOG*

Translated by
Dorian Rottenberg

Wow, this is absolutely impossible!
I'll be anger-bitten all over soon.
I'm angry, but not like you with your scowl;
like a dog at the face of the bare-browed moon
At all and every I'd howl.

Nerves, perhaps...
I'll go,
take a stroll...
But in the street, too, no one can soothe me.
Good evening! passing me, shouts a woman.
An acquaintance...
Got to say something;
I want to,
but can't, like a human.

It's simply disgraceful.
Am I sleeping or what?
I feel myself over:
the same as before.
The face I've been used to—
so why all this fuss?
Then I touch my lip—
from beneath it, lor',
a tusk!

Hurry! I cover my face as if sneezing
and dash, double-quick, on my homeward trail,
taking care to avoid policemen
But suddenly,
deafening:
"Constable!
A tail! "

*English translation
©
Raduga Publishers 1985

I stretch out a hand and freeze, stock-still.
Tusks are nothing compared to this.
I hadn't noticed it, running:
from under my jacket
a huge tail—whisk! —
trails behind me,
enormous, canine.

What now?
One yelled, then, the crowd expanding,
a second came, a third and a fourth.
An old gran got crushed
as she crossed herself, on the sidewalk standing,
on something about the devil holding forth.

And when, sticking broom-like whiskers into my face,
the mob raged around me, huge by now,
I stood down on all fours—
disgrace or no disgrace—
and began to bark:
bow-grr-bow-wow-wow!

(1915)

AN ODE TO JUDGES

*Translated by
Dorian Rottenberg*

Convicts row their galley along
over the sea in a sweltering crew
covering the chain-clang with a snarling song
about their home—Peru.

About Peru, the flower of the planet
full of dances, birds and love,
where blossoms crown the green pomegranate
and baobabs reach to the sky above.

Bananas! Pineapples! Joy galore!
Wine in sealed bottles shining through...
But then, God knows where from and what for,
judges overran poor Peru.

They came along and imposed their bans
on birds, dances and Peruvians' sweethearts;
the judges' eyes glinted like old tin cans
picked up by pavement sweepers.

A peacock painted orange and blue
was caught by their eye, as strict as Lent;

a moment, and off through its native Peru
with his tail bleached white, the peacock went.

It's said in the prairies there once had been
wee little birds—colibri they're called.
Well, the judges caught them and shaved them

clean,

down, feathers and all.

In none of the valleys today will you find
live volcanoes, those wheezy croakers;
the judges choked them by putting up signs:
"VALLEY FOR NON-SMOKERS".

Even my poems, by the law's letter
are banned in Peru. What for, do you think?
The judges, you see, declared them "no better
than alcoholic drink".

Shaking the equator, chain-gangs trudge...
Poor peopleless, birdless Peru!
Only, scowling under the penal code, a judge
survives, hearty and well-to-do.

Those galleys—things could scarcely be worse!
I pity Peruvians! Don't you?
Judges are a bane for dances and birds,
for me, for you, for Peru.

(1915)

TO ALL AND EVERYTHING*

*Translated by
Irina Zheleznova*

No.
It can't be.
No!
You, too, beloved?
Why? What for?
Darling, look—
I came,
I brought flowers,
but, but... I never took
silver spoons from your drawer!

Ashen-faced,
I staggered down five flights of stairs.
The street eddied round me. Blasts. Blares.
Tires screeched.

It was gusty.
The wind stung my cheeks.
Horn mounted horn lustfully.

Above the capital's madness
I raised my face,
stern as the faces on ancient icons.
Sorrow-rent,
on your body as on a death-bed, its days
my heart ended.

You did not sully your hands with brute murder.
Instead,
you let drop calmly:
"He's in bed.
There's fruit and wine
on the bedstand's palm."

Love!
You only existed in my inflamed brain.
Enough!
Stop this foolish comedy
and take notice:
I'm ripping off
my toy armour,
I,
the greatest of all Don Quixotes!

Remember?
Weighed down by the cross,
Christ stopped for a moment,
weary.
Watching him, the mob
yelled, jeering:
"Get movin', you clod! "

That's right!
Be spiteful.
Spit upon him who begs for a rest
on his day of days,
harry and curse him.
To the army of zealots, doomed to do good,
man shows no mercy!

That does it!

I swear by my pagan strength—
gimme a girl,
young
eye-filling,
and I wont't waste my feelings on her.

I'll rape her
and spear her heart with a gibe willingly.

An eye for an eye!

A thousand times over reap of revenge the crops!
Never stop!
Petrify, stun,
howl into every ear:
"The earth is a convict, hear,
his head half shaved by the sun! "

An eye for an eye!

Kill me,
bury me—
I'll dig myself out,
the knives of my teeth stone-honed.
A lone,
snarling dog,
under the plank-beds of barracks I'll crawl,
rushing out to bite feet that smell
of sweat and of market-stalls!

You'll leap from bed in the night's early hours.
"Moo! " I'll roar.
Over my neck,
a yoke-savaged sore,
tornadoes of flies
will rise.
I'm a white bull over the earth towering!

Into an elk I'll turn,
my horns-branches entangled in wires,
my eyes red, bloody.
A hunted down beast brought to bay,
I'll stand relentlessly,
facing the world entire.

Man can't escape!
Filthy and humble,
a prayer mumbling,
he lies on cold stone.
What I'll do is paint
on the tsar's gate
the face of Razin[50]
over God's own.

Dry up, rivers, stop him from quenching his thirst! Scorn him!
Don't waste your rays, sun! Glare!
Let thousands of my disciples be born
to trumpet anathemas on the squares!

And when at last there comes,
stepping onto the peaks of the ages,
chillingly,
the last of their days,
in the black souls of anarchists and killers
I, a gory vision, will blaze!

It's dawning.
The sky's mouth stretches out more and more,
it drinks up the night
sip by sip, thirstily.
The windows send off a glow.
Through the panes heat pours.
The sun, viscous, flows down onto the sleeping city.

O sacred vengeance!
Lead me again
above the dust without
and up the steps of my poetic lines.
This heart of mine,
full to the brim,
in a confession
I will pour out.

Men of the future!
Who are you?
I must know. Please!
Here am I,
all bruises and aches,
pain-scorched...
To you of my great soul I bequeath
the orchard.

(1916)

LILY DEAR! IN LIEU OF A LETTER[51]

Translated by
Dorian Rottenberg

The room's a chapter of Kruchonykh's Inferno.[52]
Air
gnawed out by tobacco smoke.
Remember—
at the window,
for the first time,
burning,
with tender frenzy your arms I'd stroke?
Now you're sitting there,
heart in armour;
a day,

and perhaps,
I'll be driven out,
To the bleary hall:
let's dress: be calmer,
crazy heart, don't hammer so loud!
I'll rush out, raving,
hurl my body into the street,
slashed by despair from foot to brow.
Don't,
don't do it,
darling,
sweet!
Better say goodbye right now.
Anyway,
my love's a crippling weight
to hang on you
wherever you flee.
Let me sob it out
in a last complaint,
the bitterness of my misery.
A bull tired out by a day of sweat
can plunge into water,
get cooled and rested.
For me
there's no sea but your love,
and yet
from that even tears can't wrest me a respite.
If a weary elephant wants some calm,
lordly, he'll lounge on the sun-baked sand.
I've
only your love
for sun and balm,
yet I can't even guess who'll be fondling your hand.
If a poet were so tormented
he might
barter his love for cash and fame.
For me
the world holds no other delight
than the ring and glitter of your dear name.
No rope will be noosed,
no stairwell leapt in,
nor will bullet or poison take my life.
No power over me,
your glance excepting,
has the blade of any knife.
Tomorrow you'll forget
it was I who crowned you,
I
who seared out a flowering soul.
The pages of my books will be vortexed
around you

by a vain existence's carnival whirl.
Could my words,
dry leaves that they are but,
· detain you
with throbbing heart?

Ah,
let the last of my tenderness carpet
your footfall as you depart!

Petrograd
26 May 1916

FED UP

Translated by
Dorian Rottenberg

Couldn't sit home.
Annensky, Tyutchev, Fet...[53]
Driven by boredom
again among people to roam
I go
to cinema, pub, café.

At table.
An aura of hope seems to shine.
One beat my silly heart misses.
What if
the past week has so altered this silly countryman of mine,
that I'll scorch off his cheeks with kisses?

Cautious, I lift up my eyes, peer about,
digging into the jacketed populace.
"Back out!
Back out!
BACK OUT! "
yells tear from my heart,
overrunning my face, moody and hopeless.

Unheeding,
here's what my eyes abut on:
a little to the right, unheard-of, unseen,
thoroughly absorbed in a leg of mutton,
the most puzzling creature there's ever been.

You look and marvel—is it eating or not?
You watch and wonder—does it breathe or not?
Five feet of pinkish, featureless dough,
not so much as a tag in a convenient spot.

Only, lolling on the shoulders, sleek silk bladders,
glistening cheeks all space annex.
Raging and tearing, my heart yells madder,
"Back out, now!
What next?"

I swing to the left: mouth-agape;
then again to the right, in opinion flinching.
To the observer of the second wry shape,
the first
seems the double of Leonardo da Vinci.

No humans! Can you comprehend
the outcry of a thousand days' pain?
The soul doesn't want to go dumb till the end,
yet to whom complain?

I'll fling myself down,
rub my face raw
on the curbstone, washing it from my hot tears' font,
with love-thirsty lips plant a thousand kisses and more
on the tram's intelligent front.

Home I'll go,
to the wallpaper cling.
Where else are roses more worth my wooing?
Dear, blotchy thing,
shall I read you *Plain as Mooing?*[54]

FOR HISTORY

When all are accommodated in heaven and hell,
accounts drawn up for both saint and retrograde,
in the year 1916—
remember well—
handsome people vanished from Petrograd.

(1916)

THE CHEAP SALE*

Translated by
Dorian Rottenberg

*English translation
©
Raduga Publishers 1985

Whether I'm entangling a woman in a touching romance
or just watching somebody pass—
each holds his pocket, so I shouldn't pick it by chance.
Silly!
Beggars,
what can you offer,
I ask?

How many years must go be before
they discover
that I, a candidate for three yards in the city morgue, am
infinitely rich—even more
than any Pierpont Morgan.

After so many, so many years—
in a word, I won't survive until then—
whether I starve
or make quits with a gun—
me, singer of Today,
professors will study
in every item and feature:
how,
where,
and when I was begot.
Yes, from a rostrum
some fat-head of the future
will gabber about a half-devil, half-god.
The crowd will bow low,
cringe,
full of vanity.
You won't even recognize
is it me or not?
My balded pate with habitual inanity
they'll depict with an aura or horns on top.

Each college-girl, bedtime drawing nigh,
will drool o'er my poems in ecstasy pure.
In one thing at least a pessimist am I:
there'll always be college-girls on earth,
I'm sure.

Listen:

all that my soul possesses—
go, measure the wealth in which it abounds—
my immortality itself, without limits or bounds
which, thundering through the ages, however distant,
genuflectors in worldwide assembly will convene—
all this,
if you wish,
I'll exchange
this instant
for a single word,
kindly,
humane...

Men!

V. MAYAKOVSKY

66

Raising street-dust, trampling rye,
from all over the earth throng along.
Today in Petrograd
on Nadezhdinskaya
I
will be auctioning
the most precious of crowns
for a song:
for a human word!
Dirt-cheap, you'll admit.
But there—
just try and find
it!

(1916)

TO HIS OWN BELOVED SELF
THE AUTHOR DEDICATES THESE LINES*

Translated by
Irina Zheleznova

Four.
Ponderous. The chimes of a clock.
"Unto Caesar... Unto God..."
But where's
someone like me to dock?
Where'll I find a lair?

Were I
like the ocean of oceans little,
on the tiptoes of waves I'd rise;
a tide, I'd strain to caress the moon.
Where to find someone to love
of my size,
the sky too small for her to fit in?

Were I poor
as a multimillionaire,
it'd still be tough.
What's money for the soul?—
thief insatiable.
The gold
of all the Californias isn't enough
for my desires' riotous horde.

I wish I were tongue-tied,
like Dante or Petrarch,
able to fire a woman's heart,
reduce it to ashes with verse-filled pages!
My words

and my love
form a triumphal arch:
through it, in all their splendour,
leaving no trace, will pass
the inamoratas of all the ages!

Were I
as quiet as thunder,
how I'd wail and whine!
One groan of mine
would start the world's crumbling cloister shivering.
And if
I'd end up by roaring
with all of its power of lungs and more—
the comets, distressed, would wring their hands
and from the sky's roof leap in a fever.

If I were dim as the sun,
night I'd drill
with the rays of my eyes,
and also
all by my lonesome,
radiant self
nourish the earth's shrivelled bosom.

On I'll pass,
dragging my huge love behind me.
On what
feverish night, deliria-ridden,
by what Goliaths was I begot—
I, so big
and by no one needed?

(1916)

REVOLUTION

(A POET'S CHRONICLE)*

Translated by
Dorian Rottenberg

February 26. Drunken soldiers, mixed with police, shot
at the people.

27th
Red, long-protracted,
daybreak burned,
spilled on the glitters of barrel and blade.
In musty barracks,
sober,

*English translation
©
Raduga Publishers 1985

stern,
the Volynsky regiment prayed.

5*

To their cruel soldier God
bringing their oath,
they beat the floor with one many-browed head,
hands clenched into steel by seething wrath,
blood kindling, through temples by anger sped.

The first
who ordered
"Shoot for the famine! "
got a bullet to stop up his yapping mouth.
Someone's—"Attention! "
was stabbed short,
damn 'im.
The companies' storm into town broke out.

9 o'clock

At our permanent place
in the Automobile School
we stand,
squeezed in by the barracks fence.
Sunrise extends,
with doubt pricks the soul,
scary, yet gladdening with fore-sense.

To the window!
I see—
from where heavens are pierced
by the palaces' outline sharp-toothed,
soars monarchy's eagle,
blacker,
more fierce,
more eagle-like in truth.

And instantly
people,
horses,
street-lamps,
buildings
and my barracks
by the hundred,
are hurled into the streets
in crowds.
Split by their step, rings the roadway under them,
crushing the ears, the giant stride sounds.

And then,
from the singing of crowds—
who knows?—
or the guardsmen's bugle-brass, ready to bust,
not hand-made,

an image,
glowing,
arose,
its brilliance breaking through the dust.

Wider and wider its wings' rounded span.
More wanted than bread,
more thirsted for than water,
here it comes:
"Citizens, to arms—every woman and man!
To arms, citizens, do not falter! "

On the wings of flags
in a force hundred-headed
aloft it flew from the city's maw,
the two-headed body of the eagle dreaded
with the teeth of its bayonets dashing to gnaw.

Citizens!
Today topples your thousand-year-old *Before.*
Today the foundations of worlds are revised.
Today,
to the very last coat-button, you're
to start remodelling everyone's lives.

Citizens!
This is the first day of the workers' deluge.
We come
to the aid of the muddled-up world.
Let crowds rock the skies with their stamp and yelling!
Let the anger of navies by sirens be snarled!

Beware, two-headed one!
Surging, the singing
intoxicates the crowds like an avalanche en route.
The squares seethe.
In a tiny Ford swinging,
on, overtaking the bullets' pursuit,
we tear through the city with blast-like hoot.

Fog.
The street-rivers send up smoke.
Like a dozen great barges on stormy days
over barricades manned by the riotous folk,
thundering, soars the *Marseillaise.*

The first day's fiery cannon-ball,
whizzing, rolled down past the dome of the Duma.[55]
A new dawn's new shudder gripping our soul,
new doubts assail us, delirious, gloomy.

What's to come?
Will we dump them out of the windows,
or sprawling idle upon wooden bunks
wait till the monarch
makes Russia all hideous
with graves like eerie humps?

I deafen my heart with a piercing gunshot.
Further,
mid trench-coats entrenched.
Spattering buildings, machine-guns start gushing.
The city's burning,
asunder
by cannonade thunder wrenched.

Everywhere flame-tongues.
Soaring, then sprawling.
Soaring anew, with sparks wide-brushing.
It is the streets,
each red flags hauling—
red flames appealing to Russians, to Russia.

Again,
oh, again
let your reason gleam,
O speaker red-tongued and red-lipped!
Squeeze the sun's and the moon's bright beams,
thousand-handed Marat, in your vengeful grip!

Die, two-headed one!
Into the doors of jails
break,
with nails clawing out their rust!
Shot down, like bundles of eagle-quills,
gendarmes drop in the dust.

It surrenders, the capital's burning carcass.
Through attics the search is spread.
The moment's near.
On Troitsky Bridge marches
the soldier-crowd, forging ahead.

Creaks rise from shuddering foundations and braces.
Coming to grips, at the foe we hammer.
A second,
and into the sunset's varnished embraces,
from Petropavlovskaya's bastions[56]
flame-like, soars Revolution's banner.

Perish, two-headed one!
Chop heads off!

Slit necks!
Let it never walk over us all
roughshod!
There,
see it fall!
At the last one from round the corner it grabs.
God!
Take four thousand more souls in your fold!

Enough!
All voices rise to rejoice without end.
What's God to us
with his haven blessed?
We ourselves
our dead
with the saints will lay to rest.

Why doesn't anyone sing?
Or, gory,
have Siberian cerements strangled our souls?
We've gained victory!
Glory,
glory to us, one and all!

While hands on weapons remain still clasped,
we impose a new law for men to live by.
New commandments we bring to the earth at last—
from our own grey Mount Sinai.

To us, denizens of the planet Earth
each denizen of Earth is kin most near,
whether miner,
clerk
or farmer.
On earth we're all of us soldiers here—
one life-creating army!

The flight of planets,
the life of states
are subject to our will.
Ours is the earth,
ours the air,
the stars which like diamonds the heavens fill.
And we'll never—
never! —
let anyone—
by our souls
we swear—
blast our planet with cannon-balls
or tear
with sharp-whetted spears
our air.

Whose black anger
split the planet in two?
Who raised black smoke
over battlefields glowing?
Is one sun
not enough
for all of you?
Is one sky
not enough for all—
born and growing?

The last guns thunder in arguments bloody.
At arsenals,
the last bayonet's made.
We'll make all soldiers
scatter their powder,
we'll share out to children
the balls of grenades.

No cowards' howls come from trench-coats grey,
no cries born by famine hitting hard.
The people—enormous—thunders today:
"We believe
in the greatness of the human heart! "

Where dust rises dense
over battlefields,
over all who lost faith
in love from harassment,
today ascends,
unbelievably real
all-time socialists' glorious heresy!

17 April 1917

TO ANSWER!

*Translated by
Dorian Rottenberg*

It roars and it rattles, the war's big drum,
demanding live meat to be spitted on iron.
Slave after slave
from all countries come
to handle the steel their fellows die on.
What for?
The earth trembles,
unclothed,
unfed;
man splashes in the bloody bath like a zany.
Only that somebody

somewhere
should get
his pocketful of Albania.
Human packs grapple with bloodthirsty yells,
slash after slash the earth's hide flay,
just
for somebody's ships
to pass the Dardanelles
free
of pay.
Soon
the earth
won't have a rib left whole.
They'll tear out her soul, too,
mauling and maiming her
for the only purpose that somebody should
                                                haul
in
a netful of Mesopotamia.
In the name of what,
roughshod,
boots through the cities crash?
Who's in the sky of battle?
Liberty?
God?
Cash!
You, whose life is their sacrifice,
when will you rise,
upright and mighty,
and fling your query right in their face:
WHY
ARE
WE FIGHTING?

(1917)

OUR MARCH

Translated by
Dorian Rottenberg

Beat the squares with tramp of rebels!
Higher, ranges of haughty heads!
We'll wash the world with a second deluge,
Now's the hour whose coming it dreads.

Too slow, the wagon of years,
The oxen of days—too glum.
Our god is the god of speed,
Our heart—our battle-drum.

Is their gold diviner than ours?
What wasp of a bullet us can sting?
Songs are our weapons, our power of powers,
Our gold—our voices; just hear us sing!

Meadow, lie green on the earth!
With silk our days for us line!
Rainbow, give colour and girth
To the fleet-foot steeds of time.

The heavens grudge us their starry glamour.
Bah! Without it our songs can thrive.
Hey there, Ursus Major, clamour
For us to be taken to heaven alive!

Sing, of delight drink deep,
Drain spring by cups, not by thimbles.
Heart, step up your beat!
Our breasts be the brass of cymbals!

1917

CLOUDS UP TO TRICKS

Translated by
Dorian Rottenberg

High
   in the sky
      sailed clouds.
Just four of them—
      none of your crowds.
From the first to the third
      they looked men,
while the fourth
     was a camel.
        Then,
when they were well adrift,
they were joined   •
     on the way
       by a fifth,
from which,
    absolutely irrelevant,
ran elephant
    after elephant.
Till—
   perhaps a sixth
      came and gave them a scare—
the clouds
    all vanished
      into thin air.

And after them,
       champing the clouds into chaff,
galloped the sun,
       a yellow giraffe.

(1917–1918)

HUMANE TO HORSES

*Translated by
Dorian Rottenberg*

Hoofs plod
seeming to sing,
Grab.
Rib.
Grub.
Rob.
Ice-shod,
wind a-swing,
the street skidded.
On the roadway a cob
toppled,
and immediately,
loafer after loafer,
sweeping the Kuznetsky
with trousers bell-bottomous,
came mobbing.
Laughter rang over and over,
"Horse flopped!
Boo, hippopotamus! "
The Kuznetsky guffawed.
Only I
didn't mix my voice in the bestiality.
I came up, glimpsed in the horse's eye:
the street, up-turned,
swam in all its reality.
I came up and saw
huge drop after drop
roll down the muzzle,
hide in the growth...
And an animal anguish
I couldn't stop
spilled out of me, rippling,
and flooded us both.
"Now, don't, please, horsie!
You know what remorse is?
They're human,
but why do you suppose you're worse?
Pet,
we're all of us a little bit horses,

each of us in his own way's a horse."
Perhaps she didn't need a nurse, old naggie,
perhaps even laughed at my words
—too trite! —
but the horse made an effort,
heaved,
up-dragging,
neighed, and went on,
all right.
Tail a-swishing,
great big baby,
she came light-hearted,
back to her stall,
and she felt a colt—just two years, maybe—
and life worth living despite it all.

(1918)

ORDER OF THE DAY TO THE ARMY OF ARTS*

Translated by
Dorian Rottenberg

Old geezers in moss-grown brigades
drool the same drool as of old.
Comrades,
off to the barricades,
barricades of hearts and souls!
Only he is a communist worth the name
who burns the last bridge to retreat.
Futurists, leave off waddling, lame,[57]
into the future—leap!
To build a steam-engine's no sensation:
just screw on wheels and whizz off on your train!
But if there's no song to storm the station,
what's electricity worth, explain?
Pile sound upon sound
and forward,
whistling, page after page.
There's still good consonants to be found:
R.
S.
H.
It isn't enough to line up in pairs
in pants red-ribboned and stiff with starch.
No sovdep'll make armies go anywhere[58]
if musicians don't make up a march.
Drag pianos out into the streets,
Drums with boat-hooks from windows dash.
Smash pianos and drums into smithereens,
let there be thunder—

Slam!
Bang!
Crash!
No fun
to tinker at factories,
your face in coke-soot smearing,
and then, after work, at another's luxury
to blink with eyeballs bleary.
Enough of pennyworth truths!
Old trash from your hearts erase!
Streets for paint-brushes we'll use,
our palettes—squares with their wide-open space.
Revolution's days have yet to be sung
by the thousand-page book of time.
Into the streets, the crowds among,
futurists,
drummers,
masters of rhyme!

(1918)

LEFT MARCH
(FOR SAILORS)*[59]

Translated by
Dorian Rottenberg

March, march out to the fore!
Away with speech-making lousy!
Quieter, orators!
You
have the floor,
Comrade Mauser! [60]
Too long we've lived by the laws
Adam and Eve left.
Run down old History's horse!
Left!
Left!
Left!

Ahoy, blue blouses!
Steer forth
over the roaring ocean.
Steam away, dreadnoughts!
Or
have your keels gone blunt without motion?
Let the British lion brandish
his crown,
and roar till he's dumb and deaf.
The Commune will never be vanquished.
Left!
Left!
Left!

There
beyond mountains of woe,
a land of sunshine spreads wide.
Past famine,
past martyrdom—go
crashing, million-strong stride!
Let hirelings by war-lords sent
surround us for murder and theft.
Russian fall under the Entente?61
Left!
Left!
Left!

Eagle eyes to be blurred?
Us to gaze back at the past?
Round the throat of the world
proletarian fingers, clinch fast!
Chest for'ard! Show 'em your might!
Let the sky by banners be cleft!
Who starts to march with the right?
Left!
Left!
Left!

(1918)

ODE TO THE REVOLUTION*

*Translated by
Dorian Rottenberg*

To you,
whistled at,
jeered at by artillery,
to you,
slashed by vicious-tongued bayonets' blows,
I exultantly raise
over all the vile hollering
this ode's
ceremonial
"O's".
O bestial!
O childish!
O penniworth!
O great!
What epithets haven't been piled on your doings?
Double-faced, how will you turn out yet?
As a splendid edifice
or a heap of ruins?
To the engine-driver
in soot-clouds dense,

*English translation
©
Raduga Publishers 1982

to the miner, boring through ore-bed layers,
reverently
you burn your incense,
glorifying man's labour.
And tomorrow
St. Basil
Cathedral's rafters
rear in vain, imploring your mercy,
while your boar-faced six-inchers
roar with devilish laughter,
into the Kremlin's millennia bursting.
The *Slava*,
its sirens half-choked, screaming,
wheezes on its life's last cruise.
To the sinking cruiser
you send your seamen,
where a kitten,
forgotten,
mews.
And after,
a mob with drunken shouts,
mustachios twisted in bravado coarse,
you drove grey-haired admirals with rifle butts
head-down from the bridge in Helsingfors.
Yesterday's wounds are still licked and nursed,
yet again blood from fresh-cut arteries shines.
From the philistine comes
"O, be thrice accursed! "
and from me,
a poet,
"Thrice blessed be, sublime! "

(1918)

AN AMAZING ADVENTURE OF VLADIMIR MAYAKOVSKY

(AT PUSHKINO, AKULOV HILL, RUMYANTSEV'S DACHA, 27 VERSTS FROM MOSCOW BY YAROSLAVL RAILWAY)

Translated by
Dorian Rottenberg

The sunset blazed like sixty suns.
July was under way.
The heat was dense,
the heat was tense,
upon that summer's day.
The slope near Pushkino swelled up
into Akulov Hill,
while at the foot
a village stood,

warped by a bark-roof frill.
Behind the village
was a hole;
by evening, sure though slow,
into that hole
the sun would roll,
to sleep, for all I know.
And then,
next morning,
crimson-clad,
the sun would rise
and shine,
till finally it made me mad—
the same each blasted time!
Till once
so crazy I became
that all turned pale with fright.
"Get down, you loafer! "
to the sun
I yelled with all my might.
"Soft job, sun," I went on to shout,
"this coming up to roast us,
while I must sit,
year in, year out,
and draw these blooming posters! "
"Look here," I cried, "you Goldy-Head,
it's time you changed your ways.
Why not step in for tea, instead
of rise, and set, and blaze?"
My lucky stars!
What have I done!
Corona, beams and all,
itself,
with giant strides,
the sun
is coming at my call.
I try to cover up my fear,
retreating lobster-wise;
it's coming,
it's already near,
I see its white-hot eyes.
Through door and window,
chink
and crack
it crammed into the room.
Then stopped
to get its hot breath back,
and blimey, did it boom!
"I'm changing my itin'rary
the first time since creation.
Now, poet,

out with jam and tea,
else why this invitation?"
Myself scarce fit
to match two words,
half-barmy with the heat,
I somehow nodded
kettlewards:
"Come on, orb,
take a seat! "
That hollering won't come to good.
My impudence be dashed!
Thought I
and sat
as best I could
upon the bench, abashed.
But strange to say,
with every ray
I felt the stiffness ease,
and cramped formality gave way
to frankness by degrees.
I spoke of this
and spoke of that,
about the beastly ROSTA.62
"There, there," he said,
"don't sulk, my lad,
there's things worse than a poster.
You s'pose it's easier to shine
all day up there?
Just try.
But since the job's been earmarked
mine,
my motto's
do or die! "
This way till dark we chatted on,
till former night, precisely.
Huh,
dark indeed!
All shyness gone,
we got along quite nicely.
And pretty soon right chummily
I thump him on the shoulder,
and he hits back,
"Why, you and me,
that's two, so let's be bolder!
Come, poet, up!
Let's sing and shine,
however dull the earth is.
I'll pour the sunshine that is mine,
and you—
your own,
in verses! "

The walls of gloom,
the jails of night
our double salvo crushed,
and helter-skelter,
verse and light
in jolly tumult rushed.
The sun gets tired
and says good night
to sleep away his cares,
then I blaze forth with all my might,
and day once more upflares.
Shine up on high,
shine down on earth,
till life's own source runs dry—
shine on—
for all your blooming worth,
so say
both sun
and I!

(1920)

ROT*

*Translated by
Dorian Rottenberg*

Glory, Glory, Glory to heroes!!!

But they
at the least, are never forgot.
What I intend
to talk of today
is rot.

Revolutionary tempests grow quiet, seem far.
With duckweed the Soviet mishmash gets coated.
And now
from the back of the RSFSR
the philistine's visage
pokes out, bloated.

Since the very first Soviet birthday gathering
from all over Russia, so vastly immense,
having hastily altered their natural feathering,
they've wriggled into all her establishments.

Their hindquarters calloused with five years' sitting,
as firm as washbowls and just as smug,
to this very day
they're sitting pretty,
nestling in bedrooms and offices snug.

*English translation
©
Raduga Publishers 1985

And when evening arrives
this or that trash
at his piano-practicing wife looking gladly,
his bowels from a samovar having flushed,
ejaculates:
"Comrade Nadya!
We've a holiday payrise—
something specific!
24 thousand my salary reaches.
Gee! I'll get pants
as wide as the Pacific;
Like a coral reef
I'll peep out of those breeches! "
"Me too—a frock decked with emblems.
One can't show up without the hammer and sickle.[63]
Today there's a Soviet gala assembly...
What'll I figure in there, I'm thinking?"

Marx hung on the wall
in a banner-red frame;
on *Izvestia* cosily lounged a kitten,
and from under the ceiling
screamed without shame
a canary, as if by a mad dog bitten.

Marx from his wall looked on for a while,
and suddenly, old fellow,
opened his mouth, but not to smile—
oh, did the old fellow bellow!
"The revolution's tangled in philistine webs.
Worse than Wrangel[64] are philistine habits," he hollered.
"Quicker,
wring those canaries' necks,
don't let canaries beat Communism hollow! "

(1920–1921)

ORDER No. 2 TO THE ARMY OF ARTS

*Translated by
Dorian Rottenberg*

This is to you,
well-fed baritones,
from Adam
to the present day
shaking the dives called theatres with the groans
of Romeo and Juliet or some such child's play.

To you,
maitres painters
fattening like ponies,
guzzling and guffawing salt of the earth,
secluded in your studios,
forever spawning
flowers and girlflesh for all you are worth.

To you,
fig-leaf-camouflaged mystics,
foreheads dug over with furrows sublime,
futuristic,
imagistic,
acemistic,
stuck tight in the cobwebs of rhyme.

To you,
who abandoned smooth haircuts for matted,
slick shoes for bast clogs *a-la-Russki*,
proletcultists[65]
sewing your patches
on the faded frock-coat of Alexander Pushkin.

To you,
dancing
or playing the tune,
now openly betraying,
now sinning in secret,
picturing the future as an opportune
academic salary for every nitwit!

I say to you,
I,
whether genius or not,
working in ROSTA
abandoning trifles:
quit your rot
before you're debunked
with the butts of rifles!

Quit it,
forget and spit
and spit
on rhymes,
arias,
roses,
hearts
and all other suchlike shit
out of the arsenals of the arts.

Whoever cares
that "Ah, poor creature,
how he loved, how his heart did bleed! "
Master-craftsmen,
not long-haired preachers,
that is what we need.

Hark!
Locomotives groan,
draughts
through their floors and windows blow;
"Give us coal from the Don,
mechanics,
fitters for the depot! "

On every river, from source to mouth,
with holes in their sides, river-boats too
lie idle, dismally howling out:
"Give us oil from Baku! "
While we kill time, debating
the innermost essence of life,
"Give us new forms, we're waiting! "
everything seems to cry.

We're nobody's fools
till your lips come apart
to stare, expectant, like cows chewing cud.
Comrades,
wake up,
give us new art
to haul the Republic out of the mud!

(1921)

CONFERENCE-CRAZY*[66]

*Translated by
Dorian Rottenberg*

Scarce night's transformed into dawn,
with the same daily sight I'm beset:
folks go forth to their offices—each to his own:
to glav,
to com,
to polit,
to prosvet.
Barely passing the establishment porter,
they're piled with papers like snow;
selecting some fifty—
the most important!—
to conference
people go.

You peep in:
"Couldn't So-and-So see me,
                              eh?
I've been coming here God knows how long..."
"Comrade Van Vanich's gone off to confer
on a merger of Theo and Gukon! "

The umptieth staircase.
You're done for, you think.
Yet again:
"You're to come in an hour."
Damnation!
"They're in conference:
the purchase of a bottle of ink
for the district cooperative association."
In an hour:
neither secretary
nor clerk!
Great hell!
All under 22—
blonde or dark—
at a conference of the YCL.

Again, perspiring, already towards dusk
to the top of the seven-storey building I come.
"Has Van Vanich arrived?" I ask.
"No—in session
at the a-b-c-d-e-f-com."

Enraged,
like an avalanche in full might,
I tear in,
wildly cursing.
Gosh!
Only halves of people in sight!
"Where are they,"
I holler,
"the halves that are missing?
Murder!
Manslaughter! "
I rush about, roaring.
Horrendous, the picture's driving me nuts.
Then I hear the secretary's
calmest voice: "Sorry,
they're attending two conferences at once.
At ten sessions daily
we have to appear,
so willy-nilly,
in half we tear—
down to the waist

we're here,
and the rest of us—
there."

The shock brings insomnia.
Yawning and yearning.
I meet the dawn with a dream of bliss:
Oh, for just one more decisive conference,
concerning
the abolishment of all conferences!

(1922)

PARIS*
(CHATTING WITH THE EIFFEL TOWER)

Translated by
Peter Tempest

Pounded by a million feet.
Swished by thousands of tyres.
The streets of Paris I roam—
appalled here not to meet
a familiar face or soul,
abysmally alone.
Round me
motor-cars are dancing,
round me
from the fountain-jaws
of Royal fish
jets are prancing.
I emerge
on the Place de la Concorde.
I await the appointed hour
when,
dodging the cops,
through thick
fog
comes the Eiffel Tower
to meet me,
a Bolshevik.
"They'll spot you,
psst,
don't shuffle so!"
The guillotine-moon breeds fear.
"Now listen
to me!"
(On tiptoe
I whisper
in her
radio ear)

"I've been busy
propagandizing.
Every building is with us,
But we
need you!
Will you head the uprising?
We'll vote you leader
if you agree.
Such a fine piece of engineering
rotting here
in Apollinaire moods!
Not for you
is the Paris
of bleary
bards,
stockbrokers,
Moulin Rouge nudes.
The Metro's agreed
to go with us.
It will spit the gentlefolk
from its tiled halls,
the perfume and face-powder posters
with blood
it will wash
from its walls.
It thinks:
'Why should my carriages
serve plutocrats?'
It won't be oppressed!
It finds now
our posters
and placards
of class struggle
suit it best.
Do not fear the streets!
Should the roads
block
the Metro rising,
cause delays,
the tracks will give them a thrashing.
I'll call a revolt of the rails.
You're afraid?
Of the tavern brawlers?
To our aid
the Left Bank will come.
Fear not!
I've agreed with the bridges—
and the river's
not easily
swum!
The bridges

on the Seine embankments
in fury
together shall rear,
at the first call to rebellion
shed pedestrians on every pier.
Not a thing but shall rise—
life's unbearable—
In fifteen
or twenty
years' time
steel
shall age,
and to Montmartre repairing
sell its favours
at night
for a dime!
To my land,
tower,
come!
There
we
need
you.
To steel's glitter,
smoke billowing above,
with more tender care
we'll greet you
than first lovers greet their loves.
To Moscow let's go!
There
there's space.
You'll have
your own streets—
every one!
We'll coddle you—
a hundred times
a day
polish you
till you glow like the sun.
Let
the Paris
of fops and hussies,
of boulevard loafers lie alone
in the morgue of the Louvre, mid the lumber
of museums and the Bois de Boulogne.
Come!
Stride with the powerful paws
Eiffel drew you for you to stand on,
so your brow in our sky rap out Morse
and the stars their proud airs abandon!
Make your mind up!

Rise, all as you are,
let revolt shake the city and seize her!
Come
to us
in the USSR!
I'll see to it
you all get a visa!

(1923)

WE DON'T BELIEVE! *

Translated by
Dorian Rottenberg

Its shadow out-blotting the bright spring day,
A government bulletin bars our way.

No!
Don't!
Can a tempest be bidden
                    not to rage?
No!
        Can lighting by chains be put still?
Forever and ever,
                    thousand-paged,
        Lenin's voice
                    will ring
                        like a bell.
Can thunder ever fall dumb and ill?
Can typhoons be stopped
                    from whirling at sea?
No!
        Nothing can weaken
                    Lenin's will,
Alive in the million-strong RCP.[67]
Can such fever
            be measured in degrees?
Can such a pulse
            for a second rest?
Never, never
        will Lenin's heart miss
Even a beat in the Revolution's breast!
No!
No!
No-o-o!
We can't,
        won't believe it—
                    that bulletin lies!

Avaunt,
        stubborn shadow,
                    from Spring's bright eyes!

(1923)

THE PROBLEM OF SPRING*

Translated by
Dorian Rottenberg

I'm in a dreadful quandary.
Insomnia
      isn't too far.
You see,
      soon, after world-wide wandering
Spring
      will come to the RSFSR.
Today,
      like tomorrow
            and ages before,
sunshine-drunk,
      the room goes reeling.
Work's impossible.
      I'm upset, all sore.
Though, frankly,
      there isn't any cause for such a feeling.
As a matter of fact,
      all's according to plan,
the sun will shine briefly
      and then go by.
But—
      drag the cat from the window,
            if you can!
And if an animal's curious about the street,
      aren't I!
I go into the street
      and stand there mooning,
powerless
      to shift my body from the spot.
Absolutely no idea what to do now,
Whether to move and act or not.
It's trickling godlessly
      down your collar and your nose.
You listen,
      not brushing it off.
      It's like verse.
Legally,
      you can go anywhere, I suppose,
but actually,
      it's impossible even to stir.
I, for example,
      am considered a good poet.
Say,
      I can prove
      that moonshine's an evil.
And this?
      What words can describe and show it?
All words here
      prove totally inadequate and feeble.

Say,
        Soviet office-workers,
                        dot the city!
Greet the Spring
                with a three-cheer salute!
But they've lost the knack—
                        can't greet raindrops fittingly.
Don't know anything
                    that'll suit.
Just stand around
                and gaze absent-mindedly,
watching the janitors
                    clear up ice.
Water underfoot.
                In front and behind me.
Pouring from above,
                spraying from all sides.
Something has to be done—
                        undeniably.
I don't know what—
                say, choose the best day
and let militiamen
                line the streets smilingly
and give oranges
                to all
                    who come their way.
If that's too costly,
                then choose something cheaper,
say,
    pre-school kids,
                unemployed
                        and old people
at midday
            in Sovetskaya Square
                        each day
gather
        and shout three times:
                        Hooray!
All other questions
                are more or less clear,
concerning bread
                and concerning peace,
But this
        most cardinal question
                        of spring being here
should be settled
                at once,
                    by all means!

(1923)

UNIVERSAL REPLY*68

Translated by
Dorian Rottenberg

Notes
    make me sick
when laid on
      so thick.
I propose
    without extra phrases and fuss
a universal reply
      to all at once.
If
  this or that lover
      of fire and gore
wants to provoke us
      to enter war—
we answer so:
No!
But if
    even on
      a fisticuffs'
        item
they extend a hand—
      to conference inviting,
the answer,
    you'll guess,
is always
Yes!
If this,
    that
      or the other power
scares us
    with ultimatums
poured in a shower,
we answer so:
No!
But if
    without ultimative menaces
they ask:
    "Let's pay each other's expenses! "
our answer's easy to guess:
Yes!
If
  by concessions
      and suchlike tricks
they intend
    to saddle our workers' necks,
we answer so:
No!
And if,
    reciprocally
      untying their purse,

they offer;
                "Let's go into honest commerce! "
the answer, you'll guess,
is always
Yes!
If they want
                to poke their nose
                                into our garden
on the subject
                of whom
                        we condemn or pardon,
we answer so:
No!
If
they ask us,
                as an exception,
"Pardon So-and-So,
                        he's a goof from conception,"
the answer, you'll guess,
is always
Yes!
Curzon,
        Poincaré—
                        all of us know 'em—
let them
        not think it
                        too much trouble
and read
        my little admonitory poem
before blowing at us
                        their next note-bubble!

(1923)

VOROVSKY*69

*Translated by
Dorian Rottenberg*

Proletariat,
                unchain your voices' thunder,
forget
        universal clemency's softness.
Murdered
        by a gang of fascists and plunderers,
for the last time
                through Moscow

                                today goes Vorovsky.
How many will go yet...
                        How many have gone...

How many—to shreds,..
                    into smithereens...
Some may surrender.
                    Some lose vim.
Yet we haven't
                    and won't give in!
Mould
        your wrath
                    in a bomb's great ball.
Let voices
            today
                    cut like bayonet-lightning;
become a bogy
                    for capitalists all.
On royal curtains flit,
                    spectral and frightening.
With a million feet's thunder
                    answer blatant notes.
Let millions queue,
                    serpentine,
                            by the Kremlin.
Let a comrade's death
                    affirm beyond all doubts
the deathlessness of Communism,
                    making enemies tremble.

(1923)

DON'T YOUR SHOULDER BLADES ITCH?

*Translated by
Dorian Rottenberg*

Whenever a rainbow
                    hangs down its bow
or the sky
            shines blue
                    without patch or stitch,
tell me,
            don't your shoulder blades—
                            both
begin to itch?
Don't you wish
                    that from under your jersey
where a drudge-born hump
                    used to hide,
throwing off
            the shirt's dull burden,
a pair of wings
            would go winging wide?

Or when night
                    with its nightliest stars
                                        rolls along
        and the Bears—
                    Great and Little—
                                        prowl and growl,
        don't you feel restless?
                            Don't you long?..
        Oh yes, you do,
                    and how!
        We're cramped.
                        And the sky
                            has no bounds,
                                        no border.
Oh,
    to fly up
                to God's apartments
        and show
                old Sabaoth
                            an eviction order
        from the Moscow Soviet's
                            Housing Department!
        Kaluga,
                dug in
                    among meadow
                                and grove,
        dozing
                down
                    in your earthly pit!
        Now then, Kaluga,
                        come on, Tambov!
        Skyward
                like sparrows
                            flit!
        Isn't it fine,
                    with marriage on your mind,
        swish! —
                    to wing off
                            over land and sea,
        to pluck out
                    an ostrich's feather
                                from behind
        and back
                    with a present
                                for your fiancée?
        Saratov!
                On what
                        have you fixed an eye?
        Charmed?
                By a birdie's dot?

The house where the poet was
born in Mayakovsky (former
Bagdady), a village in the
Georgian SSR. Now the
Mayakovsky Museum

A family photograph of the
Mayakovskys. 1905

Vladimir Mayakovsky's card
at the Moscow Department of
Secret Political Police. 1908

Vladimir Mayakovsky, a student of the Stroganovsky Art
College. 1910. Photographed
at Bergman's studio. Moscow

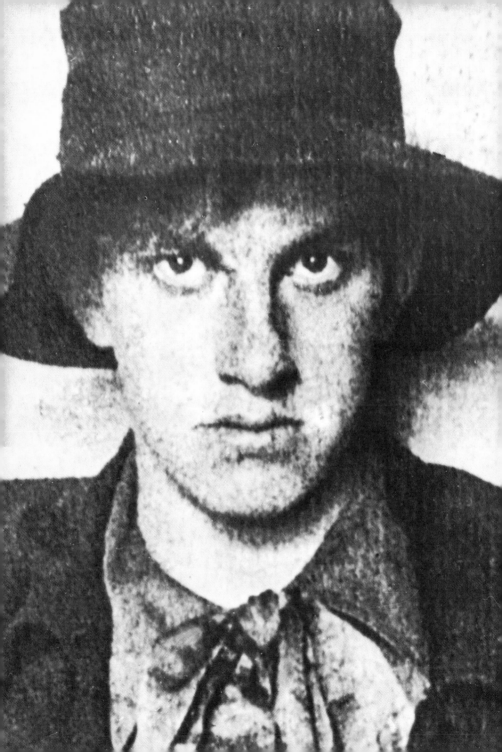

A group of futurists (V. Mayakovsky, D. Burlyuk, B. Liv-
shits, N. Burlyuk, A. Kruchyo-
nykh). 1913

Vladimir Mayakovsky in 1911

The front cover of Mayakovsky's collection *I*. 1913

Up—
    soar swallow-like
             into the sky;
it's time you grew wings,
             that's what!
Here's good thing to do—
           no deed more audacious;
choose a night
       and dash through it,
            devil-me-dare,
to Rome;
     give a thrashing
          to a Roman fascist
then back
      in an hour
         to your samovar in Tver.
Or else—
    the dawn's opened up,
          you see,
and go racing:
      who's faster—
         it or me?
But...
   all this is nothing
        but imagination.
People
   so far
      are a wingless nation.
People
   are created on a lousy plan:
with a back
    good for nothing but pains.
So to buy an aeroplane each,
        if you can,
is really
   all that remains.
Like a bird then with tail,
      two wings
        and feathers
you'll whet your nose
     all records to beat.
Tear off the ground!
      Fly, planes, through the heavens!
Russia,
   soar up
     in a sky-bound fleet!
Quicker!
  Why,
    stretching up like a pole,
admire from earth
     the heavenly hole?

Come,
              show your bravery,
avio!

(1923)

NORDERNEE*

*Translated by
Dorian Rottenberg*

A hole like a hole—
                    neither lousy nor fine...
Here I live,
          at the German resort Nordernee.
Now a ray,
          now a gull
                    drops down from the sky,
shinier
        than a door-knob—
                          the sea.
Nature's charming—
makes you feel barmy.
Now the waves
            with the tide
                          half the shoreline grab,
then splash out
              a dolphin
                        or a crab.
Now like a primus
                  they glow, phosphorescent,
then sunset
            over the sea stands rubescent.
Boy!
Doesn't it bore a chap!
How I wish
          at least
                    for a thunderclap!
I wait,
        though the waiting
                          tortures me, drat!
yet believe in it,
                  speedy,
                          believe in it,
                                        roaring;
and it seems,
              from that islet,
                                men from Kronstadt
already sail out
                and take aim from the *Aurora*.

But the sea lies meek,
                no tempests breaking,
not even
        a wind's fingers
                    tickling the wavelets.
Along the beachline,
                lazy and naked,
pressed into the sand,
                    lie languorous bathers.
Yet I daydream:
                a storm roars up from the dunes...
Bathers,
        barrels of fat,
                    you're goners!
Scram off!
            It'll cover,
                    grind,
                        blow over you
with sand-grain bullets
                    from sand machine-gunners.
But the sea
            with bourgeois heels
                        is in harmony.
The wind,
            the sand
                are at one with fatness.
With a smile:
            "How cheap things are in Germany! "
profiteers
            lie warming catarrhs and asthmas.
But there will,
            for certain,
                    come red-starred motors,
the accustomed roar
                    or red soldiers charging.
A moment—
            and into the table d'hôtes
they'll cut,
            break in,
                    springing out of their barges.
But—
        the "ober"
                    ogles
                    a lady slavishly,
the lady
        a badge mussolinian
                        displays.
Sucking
        and munching crab-claws avidly,
they watch the huge sunset
                        wedge into the waves.

Whose heart's
                been washed by October storms
wont' need
            either sunsets   .
                        or roaring oceans,
won't need
            climatic
                    or natural charms,
nothing at all,
                but you—Revolution!

Nordernee
4 August (1923)

KOMSOMOL SONG*

Death,
*   there,*
*   don't*
*   dare!*

Translated by
Dorian Rottenberg

Building,
        blasting,
                cutting to size,
boiling,
        seething,
                then calming,
it speaks and listens,
                it roars and cries,
Lenin's mighty young army.
New young blood
                to the cities we give,
new flesh to the fields,
                        new ideas we weave.
Lenin—
        lived,
Lenin—
        lives,
Lenin
    will always live.

Deluged with grief,
                to the Mausoleum
we took
        a part of Lenin—
                        his corpse.
No decay, though, can take—
                        and never will—

what's foremost in Lenin—
                                his cause.
Death,
      your scythe
                    sheathe!
The verdict
          will never deceive.
Such a soul
          no skies will receive:
Lenin—
      lived,
Lenin—
      lives,
Lenin
      will always live.

Lenin lives
          in the Kremlin's stride
at the head
          of Capital's captives.
He will survive
                and the Earth will take pride
in *Leninka*—
            its new caption.
Riots
      worldwide
              will seethe.
Through every border—
                        we firmly believe—
Communism
          will cleave.
Lenin—
      lived,
Lenin—
      lives,
Lenin
      will always live.

Let Death
        make a note
                    in that old skull of hers,
to old age
          and the grave
                        as she goads us:
"Lenin" and "Death"
                  are enemy-words.
"Lenin" and "Life"—
                    word-comrades.
Stand firm,
          however you grieve.

No ground to grief
                    will we give.
Braving Sorrow's dark wave,
whining
            we won't forgive.
Lenin—
        lived,
Lenin—
        lives,
Lenin
    will always live.

Lenin's near us—
                there, at the fore,
marching
        to die with all others
and come back to life
                    in everyone born
as our banner,
            our strength, our knowledge,
                                    our courage.
Earth,
    under footsteps
                heave!
All borders
        behind you leave,
words—
        soar up, new courage to give!
Lenin—
        lived,
Lenin—
        lives,
Lenin
    will always live.

Lenin, too,
        started from A,
                        as we know.
A genius' workshop
                is life.
From the lowest grade,
                    from the class crushed below
towards greatness
                like Lenin's
                        strive!
Palaces,
        shiver, grow stiff!
Stock exchanges,
                once firm as a cliff,
you'll whine yet
                when your behind we biff!

Lenin—
     lived,
Lenin—
     lives,
Lenin
    will always live.

Lenin
    is greater
        than all of the great,
yet even this wonder of might
mites of all times
         amassed to create—
we,
   all together,
       midget and mite.
Knot up your muscles
        tight.
Let inquisitive youngsters'
         teeth
the granite of knowledge
        cleave.
Lenin—
    lived,
Lenin—
    lives,
Lenin
    will always live.

Building,
    blasting,
        cutting to size,
boiling,
    seething,
       then calming,
it speaks
   and listens,
       it roars and cries,
Lenin's
   mighty young army.
New young blood
     to the cities we give,
new flesh to the fields,
      new ideas we weave.
Lenin—
    lived,
Lenin—
    lives,
Lenin will always live.

31 March 1924

JUBILEE POEM*

Translated by
Peter Tempest

A word, if you please,
           Mr. Pushkin.
                   The name's Mayakovsky.

Your hand!
           On my chest.
                   Look, there's no heartbeat here,
                                   but a groan;
I'm worried—the lion
                   like a tame cub is whimpering softly.
That so many
           thousand tons deadweight
                           there are in my own
disgracefully flippant head—
                   I had no knowledge.
I'm pulling you down to me here.
                   I bet you're surprised.
Am I squeezing hard?
                   Hurting your hand?
                           Beg your pardon, dear chap.
Before me
           and you too
                   the whole of eternity lies.
So
   idling a few hours away
                   doesn't matter a rap.
Like running water,
                   let us go briskly
                           babbling,
like springtime,
                   let's relish freedom
                           knowing no bounds!
Look at that young moon
                   in the sky there—
                           we can't possibly
let her
   go out unescorted,
                   roaming around.
I'm
   free
       at the present time
                   from love
                           and from posters.
On the floor the hide of the clawed bear of jealousy
                                   lies.
You can check for yourself,
                   if you like,
                           that the world is sloping:

just sit
        upon your own buttocks, dear chap,
                 and slide!
Oh no,
        I'm not foisting my melancholic mood on others.
I really don't want to talk
            with anyone at all.
It's just
        that the gills of rhyme
              are rapidly fluttering
of people like you and me,
            cast on poetry's shore.
It's harmful to daydream,
          reveries serve no purpose.
We each have
        a job to cope with,
             though it's a bore.
Life
     may surprise you though,
           and in what seems worthless
you find
      you grasp great things
          you had missed before.
Lyrics
     have had
       from us
         many a battering,
we're seeking a mode of speech
         that is bare,
            exact.
But poetry's
      a damn stubborn thing:
it's there—
      and you can't be destroyed—that's a fact.
Look at that[70] there,
        for instance,
          should you speak or bleat it?
Like the Bible character,
       old Nebuchadnezzar,
ginger-moustached
      and blue-faced—can you beat it?
"C-O-O-P-S-U-G-A-R".
Let's have some glasses!
          I know
        an ancient method
of drowning sorrow
       in draughts of wine,
           but
            see them—
the Red and White Star liners
        sailing hither

with a heap
                    of so many different kinds of visa.
You're pleasant company—
                    I'm glad we share a table.
How skilfully
            the Muse draws music
                        from your tongue!
Just what was it now
                    you had
                        your Olga saying?
No—Onegin
            in his letter to Tatyana,
                        "Dearest one,
"that hubbie of yours,
                    is a dolt,"
                        he says,
                            "an old capon.
It's you I love,
                please, positively do be mine!
This very morning
                I must have confirmation
you'll let me see you during the day some time."
There's little I've not known:
                            standing under a window,
and writing letters,
                    , and jelly-like quivering,
but
    when
            you can't cry your eyes out on a pillow
that,
    Alexander,
                is a much more cruel thing.
Come on, Mayakovsky!
                    Let's beat it South!
Squeeze rhymes from your heart—
                        why, isn't it clear
love lies in ruins,
                love's gone up the spout
and you can do nothing about it, dear Vladimir!
Oh no,
        old age is not the reason;
I'll adopt a boxing stance,
                        you'll see,
and
    take on two men gladly,
                        easily
and,
    if you madden me,
                even three.
They say
        my themes are highly personal!

Entre nous...
                    the censor will object if he hears...
There are at least
                    two—
                              I've heard it asserted—
commissars
                    in love up to their ears.
That's
          the kind of gossip
                              people relish.
Don't pay any heed,
                    Alexander, I pray!
Maybe
          I'm
                    the only one
                              truly regretting
you're no longer living among us
                              today.

I
    want a good long talk
                    now—
                              let's face it—
I too
      soon shall die,
                    fall silent,
                              and then
virtually
          side by side
                    they'll place us,
you under letter "P"—
                    me
                    under "M".
Who'll be between us?
                    Sharing our society?
In poets
          my country's
                    far from well blessed.
Look,
      Nadson's intruding—
                    what a calamity!
We'll
      get him put
                    somewhere else—
                              under "X".
As for Kolya Nekrasov,
                    the lad's quite clever
at cards
          and verse,
                    has also
                              quite good looks.

You know him, I suppose?
                    Now there's
                              a fine fellow.
He'll
      be good company.
                  Let him stay put.
Very well then. How about poets living now?
I wouldn't give fifty
                  for you—
                          why, there's nobody
won't make jaws ache
                  from yawning—
                              I'll avow.
Dorogoichenko,
              Gerasimov,
                      Kirillov,
                              Rodov—
a monotonous landscape
                  through which to plough!
As for Esenin,
              acting the peasant for us,
he's laughable.
              Like a cow
                      in kid gloves.
You read and forget him...
                  Why, he's one of the chorus!
Balalaika playing, that's what he does!
A poet
      must be first-rate
                  in life as well.
We're as strong
              in spirit
                      as Poltava vodka.
How about Bezymensky?
                  Truth to tell
he's nothing to speak of...
                  roast carrot-coffee.
Indeed
      we do have
                  Nikolai
                          Aseyev.
The fellow can write.
                  He's got a grip
                              like mine.
But a fellow must earn money,
                          it goes without saying,
your family, however small,
                      mustn't pine.
If you were alive,
              you'd be
                      my LEF colleague.

I'd give you
                propaganda tasks
                                out of the file.
I'd say:
        we need something like this,
                                do you follow me?
You'd manage all right—
                        you've got a good style...
I'd let you do ads
                for broadcloth
                                and dripping,
to get
        the women
                shopping here.
(Look, in iambic verse
                        I'm lisping
to be
        more pleasing
                to your ear.)
You'd now
        have to drop
                        those burring iambics.
Fork-prongs,
                bayonets
                        our pens are
                                because
the Revolution's battles
                        are tougher than Poltava[71]
and grander
                our love
                        than Onegin's was.
Beware of Pushkinists!
                        Die-hard Plyushkin[72]
with a rusty pen-nib
                will creep up
                                carping:
"Fancy,
        the LEFs
                have taken on
                                Pushkin...
The blackamoor!
                Daring to challenge
                                Derzhavin...[73]
I love you,
        the living Pushkin,
                                not the mummy,
overlaid
        with an anthology
                                gloss.
In my view,
        your African blood
                                meant
                                        something,

you'd seethe with anger,
                        your head you'd toss.
That bastard Dantes!
                    Society scapegrace,
we'd ask him:
                    Say *who* your parents were?
Before '17,
            your occupation?
We'd make short work of him,
                            have no fear.
Enough of such rubbish.
                        Am I summoning spirits?
A prisoner
        of honour...
                    by a bullet slain...74
Today there are still
                    many such men
                            with us
all of whom
            reckon
                    our wives fair game.
It's splendid here
                in the land of the Soviets,
You can live
            and work well, all pulling together.
Only,
    regrettably,
                there aren't any poets—
but that,
        perhaps,
                makes no difference
                            whatever.
Time's up.
        The dawn's
                    putting out bright feelers
and soon
        the militia
                will be sending out a call.
In Tverskoy Boulevard
                    we're so used to seeing you.
Let me help you
                up
                    onto your pedestal.
There's a monument
                due me
                        by rank already.
I'd blow
        the damn thing
                    up
                        with dynamite.
So strongly I hate
                every kind of dead thing!

So much I adore
                    every kind of life!

(1924)

VLADIKAVKAZ-TIFLIS*[75]

*Translated by
Dorian Rottenberg*

Setting foot
                    in the Caucasus,
                              I
                              at once
recalled—
          I'm a Georgian born.[76]
Elbrus,
          Kazbek—[77]
                    what's the other ones?!
Mountains—
                    mountains galore!
Already
          again
                    no shirts do I need—
a tramp's *arkhaluk*—[78]
                              all my clothes.
Already I ride
                    such a Karabakh steed—
swifter
          than any Rolls-Royce
                              can boast.
Long ago
          with my horde
                    long-nosed and black—
whose antiquity
                    would apall,
I clambered—
                    some nineteen centuries back
into
          this very
                    Daryal.[79]
Lezginka-dancer,
                    guitarist
                              at heart,
with long centuries' sweat
                              bedewed,
I tilled
          this country
                    as a *musháh*[80]
from here
          to Batum—
                    all through.

There's no one
             today
                    to remember those things—
lies is all
          for which History's avid:
it drones
          about nothing
                          but dukes and kings—
Iraklis,
         Ninas,
                 Davids.
This wall—
            even it
                     seems familiar a bit.
On the rugs
             of those towers
                               over there,
I recall—
           as Shota Rustaveli[81]
                                  I'd flirt
with Tamara
             in a brief affair.
And then
          rolling down
                         in a crackle of ribs,
into the Terek's foam
                       I'd dig...
Yet what's all that
                     but romantic
                                    fibs?
The queen
           played many a livelier trick!
And further I saw
                   through a rock-split's loop
from these narrow pathways
                            pushing,
down
      upon *saklyas*,[82]
                          descended the troops
of the golden-shoulderstrapped
                                Russians.[83]
Loafer,
         retreating
                     from life
                                to the heights,
to guitar-strings
                   I'd bare my heart:
"Mkhorot shen erts ratz, rom chemtvis,
Moutsia
         maglidgan gmerts..."[84]

But then
          freedom's dawn
                         all in bloody dew
far in the distance
               looms:
I,
  as Arsen the Avenger,[85]
                     too,
in the year 1905
               throw bombs.
Princelings
            as pages
                   skimmed off cream,
while I
       every day
               anew,
recall
      Alikhanov's whiplash scream[86]
as, scorching me,
               through the air
                            it flew.
And further
          our story
                  is gloomy and hard;
I see
    the governing band,
scoundrels
          murkier than the Kura,
plant kisses
           on Frenchmen's hands.
For twenty centuries—
                   maybe more—
I dragged
         the oppressors' yoke
until
     the Bolsheviks
                  came to the fore,
reviving
       Georgia's free folk.
Yes, I'm from the Georgians,
                          but not the old nation
buffeted
       into this gorge;
I'm an equal comrade
                   in one federation—
the Soviet world
               which we forge.
Though some
          of the present's days
                              may still be
marred by horrors
               of blood and fury,

we're still fermenting—
                    not wine yet are we,
no, no—
        we are just *madchari.*[87]
I know
        that heaven's
                    a stupid ploy,
but if
        it was sung about,
it must have been Georgia,
                    land of joy,
which poets implied,
                    no doubt.
I wait
        for planes
                    to soar up in these hills;
like a lover,
            one hope
                    I cherish
that we'll brand their tails
                    with "Made in Tiflis"
which
        during their flight
                    they'll flourish.
I'm a Georgian,
                but not just a saucy *kinto*[88]
cracking jokes
            after draining a glass.
I'm longing for hooters,
                    zurna-like,[89]
                            to blow
where kintos
            and donkeys
                    alone used to pass.
I give
        due credit
                to Georgian bards,
but none of the world's songs
                    are dearer
to me—
        not the zurna's or the guitar's—
than the jib-cranes'
                and pulley's
                        shairi.[90]
Build—
        with gusto,
                for all your worth,
from no demolition
                desist!

If Kazbek's in the way—
                    raze the hill to the earth—
anyway,
          it's unseen
                    in the mist!

(1924)

TAMARA[92] AND THE DEMON

Translated by
Dorian Rottenberg

These charms of the Terek's
give poets
          hysterics.
          I've never yet seen it.
                    Some loss, no doubt.
Fresh from the bus,
                    I swagger out
pooh-poohing
          at marvels
                    and merits,
poking
     my stick
               in its froth much-prized.
Fine picture indeed!
                    All decorum despised,
noisy
     as drunken Esenin[92]
                    dragged home.
As if
     Lunacharsky[93]
                    had organized
the Terek
          en route
                    to Borzhom.
Ready to scoff,
               my contemptuous nose is;
but—
     I feel I'm beginning to falter
caught in the act
                    by the sheer hypnosis
of frolicking
               foam
                    and water.
This tower
          aimed pat
                    at the heaven's heart—
deadly
     in beauty unspoken;

8*

watch it
          submit
                    to the chairman of art
Pyotr
          Semyonych
                    Kogan! 94
And,
          as I stood there,
                    I got so sore—
all that wilderness,
                    stark and abysmal,
to exchange it—
                    damn mediocrity! —
                                        for
fame
          and reviewers
                    dismal!
It's here,
          not in magazines
                    I should be
ripping the strings
                    of guitars,
not for a penny-a-line,
                    but free
to roar
          at mountains and stars.
I know my voice.
                    Not much melody in it,
yet fearful
          in towering might.
No witness,
          I warrant,
                    would doubt for a minute:
I'd be heard by Tamara,
                    all right.
Composure she'd feign,
                    though with eyes aglare,
a pretty sight
          in her lawn dress.
But I'd
          go to it:
                    the devil I care
whether you're queen
                    or laundress!
How far would you get
                    on a crooner's fee?
Why,
          laundry pays better,
                    I'd think.
And mountains—
          they don't give anything free.

Water?
     Go, take a drink!
Her majesty's fuming,
         dagger in hand,
like a goat
     by a shotgun maddened.
But I—
     I'd get her to understand:
by the arm,
     all politeness,
         "Madam,
Why boil
     like an engine
         nearing station?
We're both from one realm—
         the lyric.
I've known you for long,
     having got information
from Lermontov—95
     he's no empiric.
He swears
     that for passion
         no equal you know,
and that's how I've pictured
     your image.
My love's been long coming—
     I'm 30 or so.
Let's love
     and leave out the scrimmage.
Let's love
     so the rocks bend under,
         gadzooks!
God and devil be blowed—
     that won't miss you.
Now, what's the demon?
     Just one of those spooks,
phantom—
     too old to kiss you!
Don't chuck me down in the precipice, please!
'S not for me
     to funk such distress.
I wouldn't
     mind trousers
         split at the knees,
as to smashed chin and chest—
     even less.
From here
     a well-aimed
         slap in the phiz—
and done
     in the Terek you plumb.

In Moscow it's worse—down the staircase—

whizz! —
you count
         the steps
                  with your rump.
I've finished.
                  Now it's all up to you.
Let others
         mess
              MSS
about it
         like one of the chaps I knew,[96]
while we...
         Come, Tamara,
                       say yes."
The rest of the story
                      isn't for books.
I'm modest
         and I desist.
The demon himself
                  gives us one of his looks
and vanishes, biting his fist.
Here's Lermontov,
                  snapping his fingers at time.
He beams at us:
              "Happy couple! "
I'm all for a guest.
                    Hi,
                        a bottle of wine!
Sweet,
       fill the hussar
                       a cupful!

(1924)

THE CITY*

Translated by
Dorian Rottenberg

Two cities it is—
　　　　　　one of lawyers and barracks,
the other—
　　　　no barracks
　　　　　　　　and no Herriot.[98]
This other
　　　　brings up a lump in my larynx;
grey city—
　　　　sets my heart aglow.
From the walls
　　　　　　they promise:
　　　　　　　　　　　"Un verre de Koto
donne de l'energie"...[99]
With what wine of love,
　　　　　　　　I'd like to know,
could anyone
　　　　　stir up the life in me?
Maybe critics know better,
　　　　　　　　　I won't deny,
yes, maybe—
　　　　　it's hard to decide.
But whose
　　　　in hell
　　　　　　fellow-traveller[100] am I?
Not a soul
　　　　strides along
　　　　　　　　at my side.
As ever,
　　　　trudge on,
　　　　　　　swinging your hump
in front of
　　　　Poetry's
　　　　　　waggon.
Alone
　　　carry joy and grief
　　　　　　　　in a lump
and suchlike
　　　　human baggage.
It's lonesome—
　　　　　　forever alone here,
　　　　　　　　　　in front.

Not much does a poet need:
quick,
        time,
                give birth
                        to another one
like me,
        with feet just as fleet.
We'd go side-by-side
                on our dusty ways.
One wish eats my heart,
                by the devil! —
it's lonesome.
                I wish I could look in the face
of whoever's my fellow-traveller!
"Je suis un chameau,"
                on a poster-stand
say letters
        each a foot.
"Je suis" means "I"—
                that I understand;
"chameau"—
                "I'm a camel"—
                        well put!
Purple-tinged cloud,
                be quick
                        and pour down
on Paris and me
                your spray,
so that lights
                should go blossoming
                        all along
through the length
                of Champs-Elysees.
Let lights fill up all—
                the dark of the sky
and the black
                of the rain-soaked dust.
In the light
                like beetles of diverse design
automobiles
        buzz.
The very asphalt burns,
                no, scorches,
water and earth
                burn as hard as they're able
as if the streetlamps
                that stand like torches
were cramming
                the multiplication table.
The square
                looks more swell
                        than any dame.

Any city'd be proud of it,
                        'pon my word.
I swear,
        if I were
                the Colonne de la Vendôme,
I'd go and marry
                Place de la Concorde!

(1925)

VERLAINE AND CEZANNE*

Translated by
Dorian Rottenberg

I bump against the bed,
                        the wardrobe razor-edged—
each day I measure these four metres square,
into Hotel d'Istria
                by bad luck wedged
upon the pigmy
                rue Campagne-Première.
It's tight.
        This Paris life's not for us:
over boulevards
                strew your despair!
To the right of me lies
                Boulevard Montparnasse.
To the left—
                Boulevard Raspail.
I walk and I walk,
                unsparing of heel,
watching
        the sun set and rise.
I walk
        like the stencilled poet
                                until
visions
        arise
                in my eyes.
The fog's a barber—
                creating geniuses
puts beards on people
                        for jokes:
"Mr Turgeniev,
                a very good evening.
Good evening,
                Mme Viardaux."[101]
"Remember Rudin?[102]
                For what did we battle?

And you've set fire
    to my old estate! "
It makes me sick,
    this emigrée prattle!
To cafés
   from their whine
      I escape.
Oh yes,
   it's him,
     that old owl not far,
the great man
    untouched by decay!
I raised my hat.
     "Comment ça va,
cher camarade Verlaine?[103]
How come I know you?
     We all do, by God.
Now we bump
    into one another.
You've been drinking absinth here
      these forty years odd
on thousands of portraits,
     bother!
I've almost never
   read you before
and now
   you're long out of fashion.
I'd be glad—
   but can't understand a word:
translations
   are lousy
     in Russian.
Don't be cross!
    With me too,
     I daresay,
you're acquainted
    only by hearsay.
Let's chat about trifles
    met on our way
or the craft
   which to us
    is most dear, say.
Poems today
   are all rotten,
    just trash.
Good ones
   are too much expense.
With good ones
   I too
    would lay down my flesh
like you did—
   beneath a fence.

Befouling
       all his paper store
with pen or tongue
          uncurbed,
the poet
     like a penny whore
will live
     with any word.
I'd gladly give up
        my life for Today.
Huge!
     With what grandeur it glows!
You feel it—
       the word PROLETARIAT, say—
it calls for the grandiose!
One should turn oneself inside out—
              but jerk! —
magazines,
     prizes,
        haste!
When'll they realize:
        poetry's work
requiring
     both time and space?
"Face about to the countryside! "[104]
          now's the task.
Take to psalteries, bards!
         That's plain,
but I've got only one face,
       if you ask,
and a face,
     not a weather-vane!
And here GUS[105]
      holds forth
         as it often can
on issues
     too long awaiting decision.
"A poet—pah! —
      he's a mere artisan,
a private business
      without an engine! "
Stick a pin in the tongue
       of such a fool,
nail him up
     to museum ages.
No one's
     yet
       discovered the fuel
moving hearts
       through a poet's pages!

Ideas
> will never leaven on water—
they'd just get damp
> > and unfit for working.
And a poet without ideas—
> > unthought-of!
What am I?
> A parrot?
> > A turkey?
Workers
> merit
> > a serious tone.
We bards
> underrate them
> > at times.
Poets,
> before it's too late,
> > atone
for all of your
> verbal rhymes!
Our poet
> grabs an event
> > well-worn,
writes
> about yesterday's thunder...
No, bards,
> let's stride on
> > towards Tomorrow's dawn
double-quick, so our pants
> > split asunder!
They'll recount us poets
> > in Communism's garden—
which birds will trill
> > in elation?
Perhaps
> from the tree-twigs
> > Comrade Vardin[106]
will whistle
> his revelations?
We'll get at his throat—
> > we know what to do
with smug-looking mugs
> > like this.
Now I notice
> how envy
> > begins to accrue
in the face
> of my vis-à-vis.
And tears
> from Verlaine
> > drip into his glass.

He's all
           like a tooth on a drill.
Here Paul Cézanne
                   comes approaching us:
"Verlaine,
         let me paint you,
                        sit still."
         He paints.
               I look at his colours—
                                so bright!
Monsieur,
         excuse me, pray!
Old geezers I knew
                 would be mad with spite
at the merest sound
                of your name.
Those days
         one season
                   our god was van Gogh,
another season—
              Cézanne.
Today, though,
            art's
                like a fawning dog:
falls for ranks,
              not for colours,
                             goddamn!
Puppies—
       the milk's not dried on their lips,
yet from childhood
                they're mild and sweet.
They've adopted
             the glorious name of
                                AKhRR,[107]
yet go licking
            responsible feet!
They won't
         paint a portrait of me,
                             I daresay.
Won't waste paint
               on such sitters—
                             pettyish!
Why,
    isn't mine a face like the rest?
                           Yet they
draw folks
         more Central-Committeeish.
Cézanne
       left the line
                  he'd meant to begin,

all *merci's—*
            touched,
                        expression beyond.
While Paris,
            all violet,
                        all aniline,
arouse
            outside
                        La Rotonde.[108]

(1925)

VERSAILLES*

*Translated by
Dorian Rottenberg*

Post-haste,
            to the palace
                        this road once took
innumerable
            Louis'.
In the silks
            and gilt
                        of a carriage
                                    they shook
the hundredweights
                        of their grease.
And
            well-nigh bursting
                        his fat thighs' shanks,
pursued
            by *la Marseillaise*
along it,
            a crownless and pantless punk,
from Paris
            Capet[109]
                        was once chased.
Today
            along it
                        all Paris,
                                    gay
whisks
            in automobiles ashine:
courtesans,
                        rentiers
                                    after counting their gain,

Americans
          and I.
Versailles.
          My first exclamation:
"They lived bloody well,
                    damnation! "
Palaces—
          thousands of bedrooms and halls.
Tables
     and beds—
               send you reeling,
You'd never build their like,
                    'pon my soul,
though you spent all your life
                    in stealing.
And behind the palace,
               both this way and that
to freshen up things for the lords,
ponds,
     fountains
          and ponds,
               by my hat—
water spouting
          from copper toads.
All around,
          to encourage manners genteelest,
pathways
          crammed with statues.
Apollo's everywhere, as for Venus
the armless,
          whole legions stare at you.
And further,
          as lodgings
               for their Pompadours,[110]
the Big Trianon
          and the lesser.
Here Pompadour
          was led to a douche,
and here
          were her bedrooms,
                    yessir.
I look at their life—
          not new, by far.
Beautificity—
          simply shattering.
As if I'd got stuck
          in a print by Benois
or rhymelets
          by Anna Akhmatova.
I looked
     and felt it all,
               front and back.

Out of all that beauty
                    hard to forget—
        the thing
                that got me most
                                was the crack
        in the dressing-table
                                of Antoinette.
        Into this
                Revolution's bayonet
                                was driven
        when,
                dancing to songs and laughter,
        the sans-culottes[111] dragged the queen off to heaven
        to be despatched
                        via scaffold.
        I look—
                not bad though,—
                                a sight for sore eyes,
        these gardens and roses—
                                real scrumptious.
        Oh that a culture as fine
                                should arise,
        only of new,
                        machine-age
                                dimensions!
        These shacks
                should be dumped
                                in museum pavilions
        and replaced
                        by a steel-and-glass
        palace
                simultaneously housing millions,
        eye-dazzling,
                        for the working class.
        For all
                cash-and-coupon possessors
                                still met,
        for all
                still existing kings
                                in admonition,
        from the sky's guillotine,
                                like the head of Antoinette,
        the sun rolled down
                        on the roofs
                                to perdition.
        The crowd
                of lindens and chestnuts blurred,
                                        leaving
        their leaflets like mat-nap,
                        when lamplight fails.

The transparent
                    heavenly bell-glass
                                        of evening
covered
        museum Versailles.

(1925)

FAREWELL*
(AT A CAFÉ)

*Translated by
Dorian Rottenberg*

A saying
            commonly known
is that every road
                leads to Rome.
Not so
        with the Montparnassian.
He sees it,
            I'll swear,
                            in a different fashion:
both Remus and Romulus,
                            starting from Rome,
would arrive
            at café Rotonde or Dome.
By hundreds of roads
                    to cafés they jog
adrift
        on the boulevard rivers
                                in rain.
I also drift in:
                *"Garçon, un grog
americain! "*
At first,
        words, cheekbones and lips were fused
in hubbub
            and couldn't be heard.
Then words
            from the muddled hubbub
                                    hatched loose
and phrases
            were moulded from words.
"Mayakovsky passed here
                        the other day.
Lame! Didn't see him?
                    Which way did you look?"
"Who was he with?"
                    "Nikolai Nikolaich, they say."

"Which one?"
            "Bah, the Russian Grand Duke! "

"The Grand Duke?
$\qquad$ Fiddlesticks! Think I'm a kid?
He's fat
$\quad$ and bald
$\qquad$ as a bone!
A Chekist—[112]
$\qquad$ they sent him to blow up, they did..."
"What?"
$\qquad$ "Bois de Boulogne! —
'Go and do it, Mike! '"
$\qquad$ "He's not Mike at all.
Fiddlesticks!
$\qquad$ Makes one sick to hear,"
another corrected.
$\qquad$ "Not Mike, but Paul.
I remember
$\quad$ we used to sit here.
Him and me
$\quad$ and his wife, a brunette.
Ex-duchess,
$\quad$ they say,
$\qquad$ almost thirty years old."
"Whose wife?
$\quad$ Mayakovsky's?
$\qquad$ He's not married yet! "
"Oh yes he is!
$\quad$ To the empress,
$\qquad$ I'm told."
$\quad$ "To whom?
$\qquad$ She was shot by a firing squad! "
"You believed it?"
$\qquad$ another then stated.
"Mayakovsky
$\quad$ saved her
$\qquad$ for a million quid.
She got herself rejuvenated."
Then—the voice of reason:
$\qquad$ "Mayakovsky's a poet!
You're lying, misters,
$\qquad$ you damn well know it! "
"Oh yeah?"
$\qquad$ two gossips again intervened.
"In Moscow
$\quad$ Cheka confiscated Nekrasov's
works
$\quad$ at the end of 1917

and gave them all to Mayakovsky,
                              you asses!
You think it's himself?
                    All pinched, to a dot,
whole poems filched,
                    with the commas.
So he spoons out Nekrasov
                    and sells him, hot
for ten quid daily—
                    commerce! "
Wow!
        Such a bridegroom wasting away!
Where are you looking,
                    matchmakers?
Can a man
        with such a biography stay
unmarried
        and age among bachelors?
Paris,
    century-old
                metropolis,
how can you stand
                such emigrée mush?
Shake off from your ears
                    this emigrée gossip,
or else you'll choke
                    in provincial slush!
I went out, thoughtful.
                    By Jove, who may know?
Then spat.
            Well I never!
                    Phew!
Such rot can stick in some ears,
                    you know.
Not in all
        do things flip right through!
Now listen, readers,
                    if you ever read
that with Churchill
                    Mayakovsky's got chummy,
or married
            Coolidge himself—
                            I plead—
do not believe it! —
                most humbly.

(1925)

9*

LAST FAREWELL*

Translated by
Dorian Rottenberg

In a cab,
   having spent all my francs but the last:
"When's the train
    to Marseilles?"
Paris,
  seeing me off,
     runs past
in its beauty
    beyond assay.
Separation's ooze,
    well up in my eyes!
Sentiment,
   squash my heart!
In Paris
  I'd have liked to live and die
If there weren't any Moscow—
     my native parts!

(1925)

ATLANTIC OCEAN

Translated by
Dorian Rottenberg

Spanish stone
        rose in cliff and wall
dazzling white,
         jagged as saw-teeth.
Till twelve
    the steamer
         stood swallowing coal
and drinking
     its fill
        of water.
Then it swung round
       its iron-clad snout
and
   exactly
      at one
weighed its anchors
      and wheezing
         pulled out.
Europe shrank to a pin
      and was gone.
Great mountains of water
      run past me,
        thundering.
Enormous as years,
     at the ship they pound.
Birds fly over me.
    Fish swim under me.
Water
  lies
    all around.
For weeks,
    heaving
      its athletic chest,
now nose to the grindstone,
      now drunk as a lord,
the Atlantic Ocean,
     never at rest,
perpetually
    sighed or roared.
"Oh, to lap the Sahara!

It isn't so far-off...
A funny old trinket
this ship on the blue!
Carry or sink it—
what shall I do?
If I leave them dry—
in the sun they fry.
No good, these men,
too small to feed on.
O. K.—*bien,*
let them speed on."
There's nothing
        like waves
               to thrill and stir one.
To some
      they bring childhood,
             to some—
                 a loved voice.
I, though,
      see banners
          once more unfurling.
There it starts—
      the commotion—
          go to it, boys!
Then again all's quiet
      and the hubbub's through:
no doubts,
      no excitement,
         just nice and warm.
But suddenly—
      how,
        if I only knew—
from the depths
      arises
        the sea *Revkom.*[114]
And the militant spray—
        like water-guerillas—
go clambering up
      from the ocean's bed,
hurtling skyward,
      then downward spilling,
tearing
      the crowns
        of froth
          into shreds.
Then again
      the waters
        fuse into one
commanded to boil
      by somebody's power.
And from under the clouds
        a wave dashes down

pouring orders and slogans
                      in a ceaseless shower.
And the billows swear
                  to the sea CEC[115]
not to down
            their battlearms
                          till the end.
Now they've won
              and throughout the equator—
                                      see—
droplet Soviets
              their limitless power
                              extend.
The last little rallies
                    of quietening waves
keep debating
            something
                    in lofty style,
and now the ocean,
                washed clean and shaved,
for a time relaxes
                with a peaceable smile.
I look through the railings:
                        on with it, boys!
Under the gangway
                hanging
                      like a latticed bridge,
the waves' TU local
                  its wisdom employs
on issues
        on which
                ocean-destinies hinge.
And under the water
                  in business-like quiet
grows a coral palace
                  with spire and gable
weaving its wickerwork
                    to make things more bright
for the hard-working whale,
                        his wife and baby.
There now—
          the moonbeams
                      their carpet spread
as if on dry land—
                just step down,
                              go ahead!
Not for enemies, though;
                      the Atlantic's eye,
watchful as ever,
              looks up at the sky.
Chilly and still,
              all varnished with moonshine,

or groaning
and tossing
when old wounds smart,
the longer and closer
I look at you, Ocean,
the nearer and dearer
you are
to my heart.
Your tumult—
forever I'm glad to hear it;
your blue
my eyes
drink in
like no other—
in breadth,
in blood,
in cause,
in spirit,
my Revolution's
elder brother.

1925

SOME SHALLOW PHILOSOPHY OVER THE DEEPS*

*Translated by
Dorian Rottenberg*

I'm becoming
if not like Tolstoy,
then like Falstaff.
Eating,
writing,
the heat fit to slaughter...
In whom
won't a seascape
shake up the soul-stuff?
Water!
Yesterday
it was as mad as hell.
Today
it's a dove on eggs,
not an ocean.
Everything changes—
so it's just as well.
Everything's
in motion.
Water
too
has its flow and ebb,
all
at the proper time.
Steklov,[116] though,
always seeps water from his pen.

Would you call that fair?
                        Not I!
There's a dead fish,
                floating along,
                                all alone.
Finlets hang down
                like broken winglets.
Floats weeks on end,
                        dead as a stone,
just won't disappear,
                        damn singlet!
A steamer
        lumbers
                        into our field of vision,
from Mexico,
                slower than a seal.
                                We sail there.
Couldn't be otherwise.
                        Division
of labour,
        as everywhere.
That's a whale there, they say.
                                Maybe it's so.
Like a piscine Bedny—117
                        three metres wide.
Yet Demyan's moustaches
                        outside him grow,
and the whale
                wears his inside.118
Seagulls
        like years
                fly off in a row
then dive,
                their bellies
                        with fish to stuff.
Then the seagulls vanish.
                        Where do they go?
No one knows,
                the problem's too tough.
I was born,
                grew up,
                        sucked milk-bottles galore,
lived,
        worked,
                grew a bit old.
So life will go by
                like the Azores.
Not so much fun,
                all told.

Atlantic Ocean
3 July 1925

Translated by
Dorian Rottenberg

At first glance,
            Havana's the best of countries,
heaven on earth,
       no place
            could be gladder.
Flamingoes
      stand on one leg
            under palm-trees,
the colario blooms
        all along Vedado.
In Havana
     everything's
          marked off clearly:
whites have dollars,
        blacks—nil per head.
Hence,
     with brush in hand
          stands Willy
at "Henry Clay
      and Buck Limited".
How much Willy's cleaned up,
           there's no telling;
whole forests of dust,
        bin after bin.
Hence,
     Willy's hair fell out,
          while his belly,
on the contrary,
      fell in.
Extremely small is his joys' dim spectrum.
Six hours or so
      asleep he will lie,
and perhaps,
     that thief,
          the harbour inspector
will fling the Negro a cent,
       running by.
No escape
     from all the dirt
        people gather.
Maybe,
     if only they'd walk
        on their hair.
Even so,
     they'd collect more dirt
           than ever:
hair grows in thousands,
       feet—only a pair.

Past him
      ran
         the carnival Prado;
the three-mile jazzband
             clashed and flashed.
It really might come
           into brain-pans addled
that in Havana
         ex-heaven was stashed.
Few convolutions
         has Willy's brain silly,
few grains sprouted,
         few seeds sown.
One thing only
       firmly knows Willy,
firmer
      than Maceo's[119] statue of stone:
whites eat pineapples
         ripe and tight,
blacks
     eat them
        wet with rot.
White-collar jobs
        are kept for the white,
black hack-work's
        the black man's lot.
Few were the questions
          Willy's skull drilling,
but one
      would have made
          any white man gasp,
and when that question
          gripped hold of Willy
the brush just dropped
         out of Willy's grasp.
And so it once happened,
         just when it arose
in his head,
      the cigar king Henry Clay
was paid a visit
        by the most grandiose
of sugar kings
       whiter than clouds on a sunny day.
White Fatso
       came into the black man's sight;
"I beg your pardon,
        Mister Bragg-er.
Why is it
     that sugar,
        though ever so white

should be made
                by a black-skinned nigger?
That black cigar
            doesn't go with black whiskers.
It's fit for Negroes,
                whose whiskers are black.
And if you've a liking
                for coffee and sugar,
be pleased to make sugar
                yourself, Mister Bragg! "
A question like that
            won't be left unreplied.
The king turned suddenly yellow
                from white.
The king swung round
            in a hook from the right,
threw out both his gloves
                and walked out of sight.
All around
        bloomed miraculous tropical plants
and in a dense roof
            banana-crowns rose.
The black man wiped off
                on his white underpants
the hand
        that had scooped
                the blood from his nose.
The Negro
        sniffed
            with his nose hard-battered,
then picked up his brush
                daily bread to earn.
How could he know
            that with such a matter
you apply to Moscow,
                to Comintern?

Havana
5 July 1925

CONTAGIOUS CARGO

Translated by
Dorian Rottenberg

The steamer hove in,
                hooted,
                    roared,
and,
    runaway convict,
                they've chained 'er.

humans on board.
Negroes—
            the remainder.
Out of a launch
            to the steamer decks
popping up for inspection,
the doctor squints
            through tortoise-shell specs:
"Anyone got infection?"
Pimples well-powdered,
                features well-washed,
swaying and swaggering coyly,
the first class
            filed
                as the doctor watched
with smile
            urbane and oily.
From double-barreller nostrils
                exhaling
blue smoke
            in a cunning ring,
headmost came
            in a diamond halo
Swift—
            the porker king.
A yard
            from his snigger
                the stinkpipe stuck.
Go, pry into clients like these!
Under cambric vest,
                under silken trunks,
go and discern
                disease.
Island!
            To abstinence
                take recourse.
Don't let him beyond the docks.
But no—
            the captain
                salutes, in due course,
and Swift is let loose
                with the pox.
First class done with,
                the second class goes
in
  for examination.
The doctor pokes
                into ear and nose,
the picture of irritation.

The doctor sneered,
                    and the doctor scowled,
jowls
        all askew
                with spleen,
then sent three blokes
                    from the second class crowd
for a couple of days' quarantine.
After the second class
                    loomed the third,
black
        with niggers
                as ink.
The doctor looked at his watch,
                            disturbed,
"Cocktail-hour,
                I should think.
Off!
        and shut 'em up in the hold.
Ill—clear as day! "
                    he stated.
"Dirty vagabonds!
                    And, all told,
not one of 'em
                vaccinated."
Down
        in the hold
                he sprawls, Tom Jackson,
hell of a pain
            in his noddle.
Tomorrow
        they'll jab him
                        with smallpox vaccine
and home
        Tom Jackson'll toddle.
Tommy,
        he's got a wife on shore;
hair—like a soft black cushion,
and skin—
            the sleekest you ever saw,
just like
        Black Lion shoeshine.
While Tom
        went tramping
                for work
                        abroad
—Cuba's got eyes
                for beauty—
his wife
        got sacked
                for what the boss called
dodgin' her nat'ral duty.

The moon chucks coins
                on the ocean bed—
dive in
      and all ills will mend.
No meat whole weeks,
                no meal 'n' no bread,
just pineapples
            weeks on end.
Another steamer
            screwed in by its screw—
's weeks till the next'll be comin'.
Hunger's no help
            in pulling through.
Ah, Tommy don't love me,
                Tommy ain't true,
shares his mat with a white,
                does Tommy.
No way of earning,
            no chance to steal—
police
      under parasols
                everywhere.
And Swift—
        those exotics make him feel
lascivious
        as a terrier.
Old Sallow
        perspired
                under trunks and vest
at flesh
      so juicy and black.
He poked
      his bucks
            at the face, the breast—
at the moons
            with famine slack.
Then grappled
            hunger,
                that lifelong foe,
with heavy-weight
                faithfulness.
Inside
      was the clear decision
                NO,
yet lips
      broke huskily:
                YES...
Already pushing the door with his shoulder
was festering Mister Swift.
And time
        wasn't
                a minute older
when up they were whisked by the lift.

Tom
        turned up
                in a day or so
and a fortnight through
                        slept fast,
glad
        that they'd be
                        with bread and dough
and the smallpox bogy was past.
But there came a day
                        when on Negro skin
ominous patterns
                        were etched
and children
                their mothers' wombs within
grew dumb,
        blind
                and wretched.
The calendar skimmed
                        from day to day
crippling legs and arms,
eating
        half their bodies
                        away,
stretching their palms
                        for alms.
And special note
                of the Negro
                        was made
when the flock
                collected for prayer.
Pointing towards
                this visual aid
Parson Dry
                would declare:
"It's God
        who punishes
                        man
                        and wife
for her
        bringing visitors home."
And rotting black flesh
                        for the rest of life
peeled from rotting Negro bone.
Nosing in politics?
                Not my vocation.
I just
        jot down
                what I see.

Some folks
          call it
                    CIVILIZATION,
others—
          CO-LO-NIAL PO-LI-CY.

1926

TOPICS FROM THE TROPICS

(EN ROUTE FROM VERA CRUZ TO MEXICO CITY)*

*Translated by
Dorian Rottenberg*

I look:
          so here's
                    the tropics.
I breathe in life
                    anew.
The train puffs
                    without stopping
through palms,
                    bananas through.
Their silhouettes
                    like besoms
arise
          in sights chimerical:
imagination sees 'em
as painters
          or as clericals.
On every side
                    surprises
from all the hurly-burly:
A cactus-stack
                    arises
with all but smoke-clouds
                              curling,
while birdies
                    in this oven
are grand
          beyond compare,
in essence,
          merely sparrows,
by sight, though,
                    chanticleers.
And yet
          before I can get clear
the day's and forest's highlights,
both day
          and forest
                    disappear:

no warning
                        and no twilight.
All lines are blurred
                        both near and far.
Where's the horizon?
                        Try
and make out
                        which is really star
and which
                        a panther's eye.
The best accountant
                        couldn't count
the stars
                        that local midnights mount,
so tight
                        these August nights
                                        are packed
with stars,
                        you'd think they should have cracked!
No glimpse of either light
                                        or path.
Life dawns anew upon us.
Through tropics runs our train:
                                        puff-puff!
through smells
                        of ripe bananas.

1926

MEXICO*

Translated by
Dorian Rottenberg

This life—books about it
                                        were read at one go!
You'd walk
                        and tread on folk's feet.
In your hands
                        the schoolbag became a lasso,
mustangs—
                        all the hansom cab nags in the street.
A toyshop's entrails
                        grew real and grand.
When a steamship's hooter
                                        hooted—
You'd run off that moment
                                        to moccasin-land,
just pinch a ruble and bulldog! 120
But today
                        it's not just a dream any more:

mile on mile,
  the waters recede,
and alive
    lies the country
        of Fenimore
Cooper
    and Thomas Maine-Reed.
A roar of sirens.
      The water ends.
Lashed to land,
      our ship halts its engine.
To my suitcase
      packed with LEF[121]
          attends
Montiguomo Hawk Talon,[122]
          the Indian!
In a jiffy
    the tears
        my eyesight smother.
Never
    was joy so pure!
"Hawk Talon,
      hullo,
        I'm your pale-faced brother,
Sure!
Where's our comrades?
        Why are you embarrassed?
Remember:
      from flowerbeds in the street
back in Kutaisi
      with poisoned arrows
we'd shower Columbus'
        invading fleet! "
Through his teeth then
        Hawk Talon
          gloomily grated,
slowly,
    like a clock with broken innards:
"No more redskins—
        all exterminated
by the Gringoes
      and Gachupinoes.[123]
Well,
    and those of us
        whom the bullets
spared,
    whistling past
        without playing havoc,
in wineshops
      the deadly cactus pulke[124]
kills off
    for 12 centavos.

Suitcase piles
>have replaced forever
arrows
>which so many enemies killed."
So he snarled
>and slapped on his sombrero
instead of a rainbow
>of quetzal quills.
Though centuries
>have chopped off without pity
the heads of days bent low,
yet the time-gnarled stones
>of Mexico City
still tell me the tales
>of long ago.
Even grandmas of age-old parrots
>can't remember
when it dissolved
>in History's gloom;
from the ripples of a lake
>once rose the Pueblo,
a house-commune
>for 10,000 rooms.
In the lake
>lay sunken gold
>in tons;
no need even to mine it,
>sparkling yellow.
So it lived and thrived
>in its marble and bronze,
twin-sister of Europe's
>ancient Hellas.
But with whites overseas
>things which Indians don't need
were as ever
>in high demand.
Over in Spain
>a white bitch burst with greed—
Isabella,
>the wife of King Ferdinand.
Armed with their cannon,
>the Spaniards cruise.
Through palm-trees,
>through cactuses,
along this highway
>from Vera-Cruz
marched general
>Hernando Cortés.[125]
He arrived,
>and the lakewater came alight,

all
    a-boil
            with the blaze.
They fought
            for 72 whole nights
and 72
        whole days.
The redskins
            were saved by their double-faced idols
from the battering
                cannonade.
Yet, like mice by lard
                lured by noble titles,
Moctezuma[126] his folk betrayed...
In vain,
        reforging his scattered force,
Guatemoc[127]
            soaked on a lakeside hummock.
Small use against cannon
                    were arrows and swords.
Under torture
            perished Guatemoc.
And here now
        we stand—
                the Indian courageous
and I—
    our friendship from childhood dating.
He perished
        to stand here
                in bronze for ages
just over the street—
                near the Embassy gateway.
Beneath him
        the chain of centuries rumbles.
The Indian stands there,
                    bitter.
What to him
        and his co-slaves
                    the tumble
of all these Diazes,
                Huertas?[128]
The years flew past
            in a three-digit numeral.
Heroics today
        don't attract clientelle.
A trade-mark
        for beer
                became Moctezuma,
and so did
        Guatemoc
            as well.

Bourgeois
   trim everything
      to a single fashion;
all the world
    of its colour's been drained.
And,
  as the old planet's
      sole consolation,
two competing firms
     still remain.
No sun-coloured clothing,
      no yellow-tanned features...
From what slum-district
      could you now scoop,
extinct today
    as fossilized creatures,
one serape
   or guadeloupe?[129]
Riga,
  Mexico—
     try and tell 'em—
Latvia
   in a tropical dressing,
only that Rigans
     hold umbrellas
and Mexicans—
    Smith and Wessons.
Two Latvias
    at the earth's two ends...
Difference?
   Only this:
here they kill bulls
    in slaughterhouse pens,
there—
  in circuses.
And just as in Riga
    round about five,
cursing mothers
    who keep them well under check,
in Fords,
   whetting suitors' appetites,
      drive
daughters
  along the Chapultepek.[130]
And if all these palm-trees
     deck out the earth
and the feed-crop here's
     without precedence,
it's from the sun—
    just sprawl down and give birth
to bananas
   and presidents.

On top
    sit ministers
        with gems aflame,
underneath—
    plain folk
        with their bottoms bare.
No pants,
    first, because they've none to their name,
and second,
    they're things
        which Indians don't wear.
Today,
    where the city-boundary slants
Moctezuma's
    beggar-tribe
        stands
before the municipal sign:
        "Without pants
entry
    into Mexico city
        is banned".
500 beggarly tribes in the land,
while the wealthy
    one language
        talk:
squeeze out Indians
    like lemons
        with one hand,
lock 'em up
    with a single lock.
Don't let
    your struggle
        split up into tribes!
Beggars,
    stand brother by brother!
From the Mexicans' country
        worldwide fly
the uniting call
    Camarada!
Hunger's
    an expert
        at levelling men.
Indians,
    blacks
        and all,
You're kindred embers
        in the future's flame,
Aztek,
    Mulatto,
        Creole!
No one can silence
    a whole huge country.

The wealthy
          can't bury millions.
See—
      replacing the fallen Zapata,[131]
arise Galvanas,
         Morenos,
              Carillos.[132]
Sweep off from your humps
             the fat-bellied burden,
Aztek,
    Creole
        and Mulatto!
Quicker,
      over the Mexican homeland
red banner,
        soar up and flutter!

*Mexico City
20 July 1925*

BROADWAY*

*Translated by
Dorian Rottenberg*

The asphalt's glass.
          Each step rings forth.
Trees,
    grassblades—
       all shaved off neat.
Avenues
    run
      from South to North,
from East to West
      run streets.
In between—
     who on earth could have stretched them up so! —
houses
    a mile high each.
Right up to the stars
      some houses go,
up to the moon
      others reach.
Too lazy to foot it
     are Yankees and kin.
Plain
    and express elevators
        throughout.
At 7.00
     the human tide rolls in.
At 17.00
    it rolls out.

Engines
      clattering,
           clanging
               and humming,
people
     go deaf and dumb,
while past them
        other dumb people go running
and just quit chewing
        their chewing -gum
to snap at their mates:
        "Make money?"
A mother suckles a baby.
        "Don't holler! "
The kid,
     with drops from its nosey,
seems to be sucking
        not a breast but a dollar,
like everyone else
     damn busy.
The workday's over.
        Your body all round
by electric whirlwinds
        get swept.
You can take the subway
        and go underground
or up
     on the elevated railway
          step.
You can ride as high
        as the chimney-smoke's trail
or rub
     at the feet of a house.
On Brooklyn Bridge
        the tram wags its tail
or under the Hudson
        hides like a mouse.
You're blinded and deafened,
        you're going goofy,
but here
     like drum-tattoos,
        from the top
out of the darkness
        comes
        "Maxwell's Coffee—
Good to the Last Drop! "
And the lamps,
        when they start to dig the night,
I'll tell you, some conflagration!
You look at your left—
        Good Lord, what a sight!

To the right—
                    what a sight, good gracious!
Enough to make folks from Moscow
                                        stare!
    In a day
            they couldn't
                        toddle it through.
    Yes, this is New York,
                    and that's Broadway there:
    How do you do!
    I'm delighted
                with New York City,
                                I'll own,
        but—
            won't zap my cap off my crown.
    We Soviet chaps
                have a pride of our own.
    On bourgeois tricks
                    we look down!

New York
6 August 1925

A SKYSCRAPER DISSECTED

Translated by
Dorian Rottenberg

Take
        the biggermost
                    New York house,
    scan it through
                from bottom to top:
    you'll find age-old cubbyholes
                                fit for a mouse,
        a very
            pre-October
                    Yelets or Konotop.[133]
    First floor—
                jewellers
                        in unrelieved vigil.
    Locks hitched fast
                    to the shutter's brow.
    Film-star policemen,
                    grey-clad, rigid;
        hound-like they'll die
                        guarding others' dough.
    Third floor—
                offices,
                    gains and losses.

Blotting-paper
      rotting
          in slavish sweat.
So the world
      shan't forget
          who the boss is—
doorsigns
      in gold:
          "William Sprat".
Fifth.
      After counting
          the slips in her trousseau
an over-ripe miss
          lies in dreams about grooms.
Her bust
      raising lace
          whose finesse
               rouses awe,
she scratches
      her armpits'
          prodigious brooms.
Seventh.
      Having built up
          his strength
               through sport
a mister
      towers
          over the domestic hearth;
discovering
      marital infidelity
          of some sort,
he gives a polishing
      to his better half.
Tenth.
      A honeymoon-couple in bed.
Connubial bliss
      written large on their faces.
Busy reading
      a *New York Times* ad:
"Buy our cars on a monthly basis".
Thirtieth.
      Shareholders in conference jam,
dividing billions
      with snarl and scuffle—
the profits of a firm
      manufacturing ham
out of top-quality
      Chicago
          dog-offal.
Fortieth.
      By the bedroom of a music-hall beaut',

focussing his fervour

on the keyhole of the said,
to wrest a divorce from Coolidge,134
a sleuth
waits to catch a husband
red-handed
in bed.
A free-lance painter
of bare-arse portraits
dozes in the ninetieth,
contemplating
how to win the favour
at the landlord's daughter
and simultaneously
get him
to buy a painting.
Penthouse.
Tablecloth
white past believing.
Alone
in the restaurant
next to the sky
a Negro cleaner
eats sizeable leavings,
while rats
clean up crumbs
of lesser size.
I look
in a blend
of anger and boredom
at the inmates
of the ninety-storey shack.
I'd meant
to go 7,000 miles forward
but it looks,
I've been taken
seven years back.

1925

A DECENT CITIZEN*

*Translated by
Dorian Rottenberg*

*English translation
©
Raduga Publishers 1985

If
you can't
make out your enemies
lately,
if your ardour's drained
by haggling NEP,135

if you're
          out of the habit
                              of hating,
New York
          is the place to go to,
                                        yep!
Here,
          where like porcupines
                              lamp-needles sting me,
where straggling street-miles
                              leave me sore,
come and join me—
                    creep like a pigmy
at the foot
          of these storeys
                              galore.
Watch them rummage
                    in garbage messes
to keep their kids
                    out of hunger's reach,
whilst in cars,
                    overtaking buses,
off to their palaces
                    speed the rich,
Peer into one of these windows,
                              matey.
Here they sew 'em,
                    their garments sumptious,
whilst the steel of the elevated
drowns the coughing
                    of tailors' consumption.
And the boss—
                    lascivious jelly—
with a mug
          like a boil livid-topped,
pinches girls
          by the tits and belly:
"Her who pleases me
                    I'll adopt!
100 won't do?
                    200 I'll pile up,
drive sorrow forever
                    from your sweet gaze.
Your life will become
                    one big Coney Island,
one big luna-park
                    with lamp all ablaze."
He'll lead her off,
                    and tomorrow together
a wolf-pack of sexless hags—
                    ya-ha! —

will roll
                    the whore
                              in tar and in feathers,
and once again
                              in feathers and tar.
Meanwhile the boss
                              in Hotel Plaza,
toasting God
                    in brandy-born booziness,
eyes raised skyward
                              in piety's dazzle,
croaks,
          "Thanks, Almighty,
                              for boosting my business! "
You needn't worry—
                    out of harm's way
are your sobriety,
                    morals,
                              urchins.
The drums of every salvation army
proclaim to the world
                    your sterling virtues.
God won't have cause
                    to put you to shame.
From you—
          for a shawl that their Mum can put on—
and for a brand-new
                    gold icon-frame
will collect cash
                    god's manager—
                              Father Platón.136
No policeman's club
                    on your pate will come diving.
To help you batten,
                    pretending he's foolish,
at your doings
                    with fat connivance
looks
     the Democrat President Coolidge.
And,
     right up to the sky reared, dizzy,
a watchdog of dollars,
                              fat
                              and lies,
your Liberty
                    over Ellis Island's prison
pokes her hand
                    at the skies.

1925

Translated by
Dorian Rottenberg

A CHALLENGE*

Under Alps of anger
          my feet go bending.
Even my neck
          swells up in a gob.
My mouth full,
          my eyes full,
               my bowels rending,
settling,
          anger-lumps
              quiver and throb.
All on fire,
          on Riverside I stride,
high-risers
          from behind
              my elbows twisting.
Fords
          storm fortresses of darkness
              at my side,
the US Navy
          lies before me,
              glistening.
And yet I laugh
          at their triple attack.
My visa's been overlooked
          by their Nick Carters.
An envoy of verse,
          with my land at my back,
I throw my challenge
          at your States,
              me hearties!
If a single crumb
          smells of mould in your mouth,
chuck out the whole rotten bite,
              make haste!
I spat out
          after less than a month
all your achievements,
          your laws,
              your tastes.
To the deepest,
          blackest hell
              I send
all the dollars
          collected worldwide.
In the pants I began
          my life I'll end,
nothing
          in all my years
              having hoarded.

*English translation
©
Raduga Publishers 1985

We despise
                your zones
                        of the permissible.
Let our cynicism
                cut husbands
                        like knives.
By the Hudson—
                lawlessly! —
                        we go kissing them,
your delight and pride—
                        your long-legged wives.
Our days are noisy,
                our nights delicious.
Send your detectives
                to eavesdrop through keyholes!
We drink,
        spitting at your prohibition,
our daily
        White Horse
                with sneers and hee-haws.
I too
    to fraternalize
                through my poems
arrived here,
        hammering in ideas.
No deportation on earth
                can scare 'em,
nor any exile
                overseas.
Ideas turn to words,
                and words into acts
and then from
        these skyscrapers
                in due course,
swung out
        and onto the roadway smacked,
will fly
        Vanderlipp's,
                Ford's,
                        Rockefeller's corpses.
Today, though,
                the dollar's pinned poetry down.
Plundering,
        grabbing,
                pilfering,
with Broadway
        slouched on
for a legal crown,
steps Capital,
        His Imperial
                Filthiness.

1925

E. Lisitsky's illustration to Mayakovsky's "Third International"

E. Lisitsky's drawing for Mayakovsky's poem "Left March"

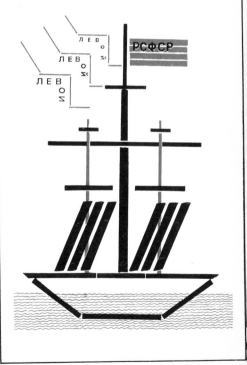

Vladimir Mayakovsky in 1918

Mayakovsky with the team of "Windows of ROSTA". 1920

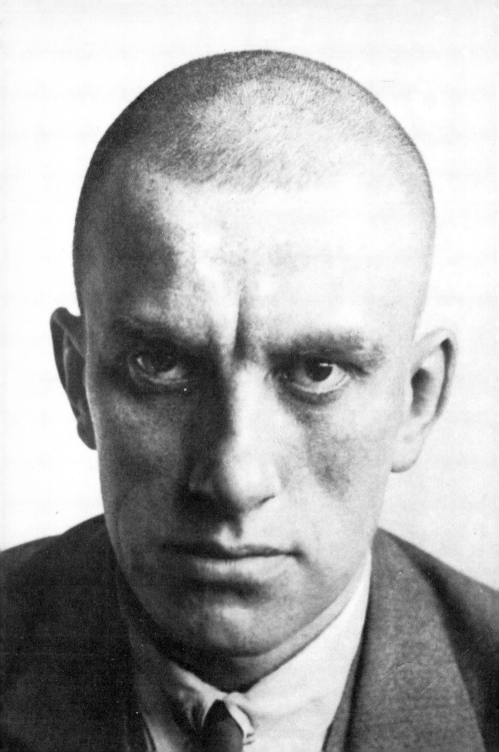

Vladimir Mayakovsky in 1924.
Photo by A. Rodchenko

Mayakovsky. Paris. 1925.
Photo by P. Shumov

Mayakovsky with his dog Skok at a country house in Pushino. Photo by A. Rodchenko. 1924

Mayakovsky. Mexico. July 1925.

BROOKLYN BRIDGE

Translated by
Dorian Rottenberg

Coolidge, old boy,
give a whoop of joy!
What's good is good—
                          no need for debates.
Blush red with my praise,
                          swell with pride
                                              till you're spherical,
though you be ten times
                          United States
of America.
As to Sunday church
                          the pious believer
walks,
        devout,
                  by his faith bewitched,
so I,
      in the grisly mirage
                          of evening
step, with humble heart,
                          on to Brooklyn Bridge.
As a conqueror rides
                          through the town he crushes
on a cannon
                  by which himself's a midge,
so—
      drunk with the glory—
                          all life be as luscious—
I clamber,
            proud,
                    on to Brooklyn Bridge.
As a silly painter
                    into a museum Virgin,
infatuated,
              plunges
                        his optics' fork,
so I
      from a height on heaven verging
look
      through Brooklyn Bridge at New York.
New York,
              till evening stifling and bewildering,
forgets
          both its sultriness
                                and its height,
and only
            the naked soul
                            of a building
will show
          in a window's translucent light.

From here
                    the elevators
                              hardly rustle,
which sound alone,
                    by the distance rubbered,
betrays the trains
                    as off they bustle,
like crockery
          being put by
                    in a cupboard.
Beneath,
          from the river's far-off mouth,
sugar
          seems carted from mills by peddlers,
it's the windows of boats
                              bound north and south—
tinier
          than the tiniest pebbles.
I pride
          in the stride
                    of this steel-wrought mile.
Embodied in it
                    my visions come real—
in the striving
          for structure
                    instead of style,
in the stern, shrewd balance
                    of rivets and steel.
If ever
          the end of the world
                    should arrive,
and chaos
          sweep off
                    the planet's last ridge,
with the only lonely
                    thing to survive
towering over debris
                    this bridge,
then,
          as out of a needle-thin bone
museums
          rebuild dinosaurs,
so future's geologist
                    from this bridge alone
will remodel
          these days
                    of ours.
He'll say:
          this mile-long iron arch
welded
          oceans and prairies together.

From here old Europe
                    in westward march
swished
        to the winds
                    the last Indian feather.
This rib will remind
                    of machines by its pattern.
Consider—
        could anyone with bare hands
planting
        one steel foot
                    on Manhattan
pull Brooklyn
            up
            by the lip
                    where he stands?
By the wires—
            those tangled electric braidings—
he'll tell:
        it came after steam, their era.
Here people
        already
                hollered by radio,
here folks
        had already soared up by aero.
Here life
        for some
                was a scream of enjoyment,
for others—
        one drawn-out,
                    hungry howl.
From here the victims of unemployment
dashed headlong
                into the Hudson's scowl.
And further—
            my picture unfurls without hitch—
by the harp-string ropes,
                    as the stars' own feet,
here stood Mayakovsky,
                    on this same bridge,
and hammered his verses
                    beat by beat.
I stare like a savage
                at an electric switch,
eyes fixed
        like a tick on a cat.
Yeah,
        Brooklyn Bridge...
It's something, that!

1925

HOME!

Translated by
Dorian Rottenberg

Thoughts, be off
            and go where you are going!
Merge together,
          deeps of soul and sea!
Anybody
       permanently
             tranquil
                 and knowing
is simply stupid,
          to me.
This berth
       which I've booked,
               it's a hell of a berth;
all night
       feet go pounding
             for all they're worth.
All night,
       upsetting the peace of the ceiling,
a dance-band blares
           and a voice goes squealing:
"Marquita,
       Marquita,
Marquita
      my dove,
why don't you,
         Marquita,
say yes to my love?"
But why should
        Marquita love me,
              really,
when I've never even
          got a franc to spare?
For a 100—
       bah! —
          just wink and she'll be willing
to accompany you home
           or anywhere.
Not so much:
       enough, though,
            to show off for.
Surer than your poet's way with girls;
a sewing outfit's all we have to offer
good for nothing
          but to stitch the silk of verse.
Proletarians
       come to communism
            from down under.

I—
            from my poetic skies above
hurtle unto communism—
                                        tear asunder
me and it—
                        and I've no life nor love.
Whether self-exiled
                                or just sent packing,
my word-steel rusts,
                                        my voice-bronze dims with stains.
Why should I go rusty,
                            rot and blacken
under these confounded foreign rains?
Here I lie,
                    gone off beyond the sea;
the parts of my machine
                                    with mildew cloy.
But why?
                I feel
                            I'm just another Soviet factory
manufacturing joy!
I'd loathe
                being plucked
                                    like a flower from a lawn
after
            workaday
                            sweat.
Let Gosplan137
                        debating
                                    from dusk until dawn
my yearly assignment set.
Let the people's commissar
                                        of the times
loom
            with his orders
                                    over my rhymes.
Let the T. U. chief,
                            when told by the clock,
arrive
            and shut
                            my lips with a lock.
Let love
                by the carload
                                        be given my heart
as a super-salary
                            for my art.
Let the pen and the bayonet
                                            stand in line,
both
            getting first attention.

Let the output of verse
                    with the output of iron
be reported
            at party conventions;
say, "So-and-so,
                comrades,
                            to the highest standing
workers have risen
                    from one-time dark.
In these republics
                    verse-understanding
has topped
            the pre-war mark! "

1925

TO SERGEI ESENIN

Translated by
Dorian Rottenberg

You've departed,
        as they say,
                to another world.
Emptiness...
      Fly on,
            with stars colliding.
No money to collect.
           No beershops.
                In a word—
Sobriety.
No, Esenin,
      this is not a sneer.
No chortles in my throat,
          but a lump of woe.
A sagging bone-bag
        in my vision
             you appear,
red runnels
      from your slashed-up wrist-veins flow.
Stop,
    leave off!
             Are you in your right mind?
To let your cheeks be smeared
            with deathly lime?
You,
    who'd pull off pranks
            of such a kind
that no one
      could have matched at any time!
Why?
    What for?
          There's really no accounting.
Critics mumble,
        it was all because
this and that—
      but chiefly poor class-contact[138]
which resulted
        in too much strong drink,
                of course.

"Had he given up
             bohemians
                        for *the* class
it'd influence him,
                   he'd have less time for fights..."
But that class—
            you think it slakes its thirst
                              with *kvass?*[139]
Yeah—
      the class—
            it doesn't
                  mind a booze
                           on pay-day nights.
If, they say,
         he had been supervised
                           by someone "at the post"[140]
he'd have got
          a lot more gifted
                     as to content.
He'd have written verse
                 as fast as prose
(long-drawn-out and dreary as Doronin[141])...
But if some such thing had happened,
                              I should think
you'd have done it—
                slit your wrist-veins—
                              long before.
I'd rather,
       if you ask me,
                  die of drink
than be bored to death
                 or live a bore.
Whether it was boredom
                 or despair
neither you
        nor penknife
                 can explain.
Maybe,
     had there been some ink
                        in the Angleterre
there'd have been no cause
                      to slit a vein.
Imitators jumped at it—
                  encore!
Dozens hurried
            to repeat the bloody deed.
But, listen,
         why increase
                  the suicidal score?
Better make more ink
            to meet the need!

His tongue's now locked
                         between his teeth
                                        forever.
To bandy words
              is just a shame
                              and waste of breath.
The people,
            that supremest language-weaver,
has lost a lusty
                 young apprentice
                                  with his death.
So now
       they bring along
                         funereal scrap,
verses
       scarce rebotched
                         since the last decease,
and line the grave
                   with lines
                              obtuse and drab.
Is that the homage
                   that a poet should receive?
Although the monument
                      that you deserve
                                       had not been cast—
where is it,
            ringing bronze
                           and hard-grained granite?—
The drain of memory's
                      already thick with dust;
remembrances
             and dedications
                             set upon it.
Your name
          is being snivelled
                             into hankies.
With your words
                maestro Sobinov[142]
                                    hanky-pankies
and trills
           beneath a stillborn birch,
                                      as if he'd die,
"Oh not a wo-o-ord,
                    my friend,
                              ah, not a si-i-igh! "[143]
Bah!
     I'd like to talk
                      a bit more briskly
with that selfsame
                   Leonid V. Loengrinsky! [144]

I'd stand up in their way,
                                  a thundering brute:
"How dare you mumble verse
                                  like cows chew cud?"
I'd deafen them—
                    I'd whistle and I'd hoot:
"Your blank-blank mother,
                        grandmother,
                              your blinking soul and God!"
So all the giftless scum
                    skedaddle off to hell,
flapping
            their inflated
                        jacket-skirts,
so P. S. Kogan[145]
                    should go scattering
                                        pell-mell,
piercing
            all he meets
                        with whisker-darts.
Riff-raff
            hasn't scarcened much
                                    as yet.
There's lots to do,
                    so hurry, mates,
                                    along.
Life must first
                be thoroughly reset,
rebuilt—
            remade—
                        and only then extolled in song.
These days—
                they are a little hard
                                        upon the pen.
But tell me,
                cripples,
                            cripplesses,
                                        if it pleases you,
whoever of the great ones,
                            where and when
chose paths
                that were both better-trod
                                            and easier?
Words
        command and muster
                            human strength.
March!
        Let time explode like gunshells,
                                        far behind,
so that back to the old days
                            the wind should fling

only hairscraps,
             twisted up and twined!
It isn't much equipped for merriment,
                              our world.

Let's wrest joy
            from the grips
                        of a future day!

Dying
        in this life
                     is not so hard,
building life
             is harder,
                        I daresay.[146]

1926

TO BRITISH WORKERS*[147]

Translated by
Peter Tempest

No trains run,
              the dock cranes are still.
Serving the boss class,
                        cops are on duty.
News reports
             down your spine send a chill
as at the dawn
               of our Revolution.[148]
Radios
        their steel necks rotate,
straining
          for news
                    from across the Channel.
Will the men win?
                  Give in?
                            Be betrayed?
Or will they greet us
                      waving red banners?
I hear,
        I can hear
                    the troop lorries roaring...
The clang of weapons...
                         The clink of spurs...
Into the docks
               go strikebreaking forces.
Sea!
      In their faces
                      with storm fury burst!
I hear
        court lackeys
                       shuffle in procession:

to Tory Baldwin,
                that blathering bloke,
Ramsay Macdonald
                goes making concessions.
Lightning!
                That compromise kill at one stroke!
I hear
        sounds of weeping the silence fill.
There's no food—
                nothing to sip or gobble.
Fog!
        Flow to the strikers
                        as fresh milk!
Turn into loaves of bread
                        every cobble!
The radio's silent,
                on strike is the sky.
Not a word
            can be heard.
                        There's not a sound.
Stop,
        Earth too!
                Don't go rushing by!
May they stand firm,
                may they hold their ground.
So you're
        not ensnared
                by those soft-soapers,
so brightly
        you blaze—
                not in fits and starts,
accept our fraternal greetings,
                our kopeks,
the strength of our handclasp,
                the warmth of our hearts.
Political charades
            we hate!
                In crappy
fairytales
        Bolsheviks don't believe.
What makes you happy
                makes us too happy.
You suffer—
        we suffer,
                together we grieve.
A bird's job
        is now what I'd like.
                I'd fly off to
London and—
        pardon my passion, my haste! —

round all five,
                    all five million of you
I'd throw
            my arms
                    in a fond embrace.

(1926)

TALKING WITH THE TAXMAN ABOUT POETRY*

Translated by
Peter Tempest

Sorry to bother you,
                    Citizen taxman!
No thanks...
            Don't worry...
                        I'd rather stand.
I've come to see you
                    on a delicate matter:
the place
        of the poet
                    in a workers' land.
Along with
            storekeepers
                        and land users
I'm taxable too,
                and am bound by the law.
Your demand
            for the half-year
                        is 500 roubles,
and for not filling forms in—25 more.
My labour's
            no different
                        from any other labour.
Examine these figures
                    of loss and gain,
the production
            costs
                I have been facing,
the raw material
                I had to obtain.
With the notion of "rhyme"
                        you're acquainted,
                                    of course?
When a line of ours
                    ends with a word
                                like "plum"
in the next line but one
                        we repeat
                            the syllable

with some other word
                    that goes
                            "tiddle-ti-tum".
A rhyme
        is an IOU,
                    as you'd put it.
"Pay two lines later"
                    is the regulation.
So you seek
            the small change of inflexion, suffix
in the depleted till
            of declensions,
                        conjugations.
You shove
        a word
                into a line of poetry
but it just won't go—
                    you push and it snaps.
Upon my honour,
                Citizen taxman,
words
    cost poets a pretty penny in cash.
As we poets see it,
                a barrel
                        the rhyme is,
a barrel of dynamite,
                the fuse is
                        each line.
The line starts smoking,
                    exploding the line is,
and the stanza
            blows
                a city
                    sky-high.
Where to find rhymes,
                in what tariff list,
that hit the bull's eye
                with never a failure?
Maybe
    a handful of them
                    still exist
faraway somewhere
                in Venezuela.
I have to scour
            freezing
                    and tropical climes.
I flounder in debt,
                I get advance payments.
My travel expenses
                bear in mind.

Poetry—
          all poetry—
                    is an exploration.
Poetry
          is just like mining radium.
To gain just a gram
                    you must labour a year.
Tons of lexicon ore
                    excavating
all for the sake of one precious word.
But
          how searing
                    the heat of this word is
alongside
          the smouldering
                    heap of waste.
There are the words
                    that go rousing, stirring
millions of hearts
                    from age to age.
Of course,
          there are different brands of poet.
Famed for sleight of hand
                    are quite a few.
Verses they pull,
                    like a conjuror,
                              boldly
out of their own mouths—
                    and others' too.
What can one say
                    of the poetry eunuchs?
They write
          stolen lines in—
                    not turning a hair.
Thieving
          like that
                    is nothing unusual
in a country
          where thieves are enough and to spare.
These
          contemporary
                    odes and verses
which with rapt ovations
                    audiences greet
will go down
          in history
                    as overhead charges
for the achievements
                    of a few of us—
                              two or three.

It takes
>>quite a time,
>>>>to get to know people,
smoke many a packet of cigarettes
till you raise
>>that wonderful word
>>>>>you're needing
from the deep artesian
>>>>folk wells.
Straightaway
>>the rate of tax
>>>>grows less.
Knock
>>that wheel-zero
>>>>off the total due.
I pay one rouble 90
>>>>for a hundred cigarettes
and one rouble 60
>>>>for the salt I consume.
I see in your form
>>>>there's a host of questions:
"Travelled abroad?
>>>>>Or spent all the time here?"
What if
>>I've run down
>>>>a dozen Pegasuses
in the course of
>>>>these
>>>>>fifteen years?!
You want to know
>>>>how many servants
>>>>>>I'm keeping,
what houses?
>>>>My special case please observe:
where
>>do I stand
>>>>if I lead people
and simultaneously
>>>>the people serve?
The class
>>speaks
>>>>with the words we utter
and we
>>proletarians
>>>>push the pen.
The soul-machine
>>>>wears out,
>>>>>begins to splutter.
They tell us:
>>"Your place
>>>>now
>>>>>is on the shelf."

There's ever less love,
                    less bold innovation,
time
     strikes my forehead
                         a running blow.
There comes
            the most terrifying depreciation,
the depreciation
                 of heart and soul.
When
     one day this sun
                      shall like a fattened hog in
a land rid of beggars
                      and cripples
                                   rise,
dead by the fence
                  I'll
                       have long
                                been rotting
along with
          ten or so
                    colleagues of mine.
Draw up
       my posthumous balance-sheet!
I tell you—
           upon this I'm ready to bet—
unlike
      all the dealers and climbers
                                   you see
I'll be
       a unique case—
                      hopelessly in debt.
Our duty is
           to roar
                   like brass-throated sirens
in philistine fog
                 and in stormy weather.
Paying
      fines in cash
                   and high interest
                                     on sorrow,
the poet is
           always
                  the Universe's debtor.
And I
     . owe a debt
                 to the lights of Broadway,
a debt to you also,
                    Bagdady skies,
to the Red Army
               and to Japan's cherry blossom—

to all
about which
I had no time to write.
Why
did I undertake
this burden?
With rhyme to shoot,
with metre anger to spark?
Your resurrection
the poet's word is,
your immortality,
Citizen clerk.
Read any line
a hundred years after
and it brings back the past,
as fast as a wink,
all will come back—
this day
with the taxman
with a glint of magic
and the reek of ink.
Come, you smug dweller in the present era,
buy your rail ticket
to Eternity
here.
Calculate
the impact of verse
and distribute
all that I earn
over three hundred years!
Not only in this
lies the power of a poet,
that it's you
future generations
will think about.
Oh no!
Today too
are the rhymes of a poet
a caress,
a slogan,
a bayonet,
a knout.
Five—
not five hundred—
roubles I'll pay
you, Citizen taxman!
Delete every nought!
As of right
I'm
demanding a place

with workers
                    and peasants
                                    of the poorest sort.
But if
        ⸳ you think
                    all I do is just press
words other people use
                        into my service,
Comrades,
            come here,
                    let me give you my pen
and you
        can yourselves
                        write your own verses!

(1926)

BRIBE-TAKERS*

Translated by
Dorian Rottenberg

A door;
        on the door—
                        "No Entry Unannounced".
Under Marx
            in an armchair,
                            smug and proud,
big-salaried,
            sleek—
                    off him marbles would bounce—
sits
a Responsible
                entitled and empowered.
In a smuggled gift-waistcoat
                            he sits in state,
in his pocket
            a fountain-pen
                        on guard;
from another—
                with a forged joining date—
sticks the barely seen corner
                            of a membership card.
All day's
            one unending job for his brain.
On his forehead—
                    the symptoms of thought are buzzing:
to whom
            to appoint his beloved cousine,

*English translation
©
Raduga Publishers 1985

to whom to offer
                    his favourite cousin.
All are his protegées
                    to the smallest fry,
everywhere
                    he has agents.
He knows
            at whom
                    poisoned darts
                                to let fly,
where to have a hand
                    for urgent measures.
Each sits where he must:
fiancée—
in a trust,
a brother-in-law
in the GUM,[149]
                    and what's more,
cousin Kondrat
in a Commissariat.
Friends and relatives
                    sit in hordes,
their sphere grows bigger and bigger.
On pay-days
            in the lists of awards and rewards
against their names
                    stand enormous figures.
He's an expert
                of a very special kind,
nothing in him
                of the mystic:
he interprets
            the brotherhood of mankind
as the welfare
            of brothers,
                        aunts
                                and sisters.
He meditates
            how to cut down personnel;
Kate's eyes
            look radioactive!
Or maybe
            give preference
                        to Nell?
Her lines
            look a bit more attractive.
Smoke-wreathes
                smother the ventilation.
Responsible shrugs his shoulders:
                                "No!
Your case
        is under consideration.

Come again
      in a day or so."
But they never seem to come,
            those days long-awaited.
In vain the applicant
        bends in a bow.
No go!
      There's not enough data!
It takes a long time
         till it dawns on him,
till, searching his briefcase
        as hinted
the applicant hands
        an envelope in
with "new data",
        crisp, fresh-minted.
With the virgin blush
        of a red-cheeked beauty,
he "good-byes",
        concealing the gift
           with his palm.
Wetting his finger,
        too thrilled to be calm,
the scoundrel sits counting his booty.
The giver,
      meanwhile,
        righteously cross,
all red,
      through the office yells:
"Bring the resolution! "
        And all across
the paper
      appears a fat "YES".
Off to a date
      Responsible whirls
in the car
      he uses
        by right.
Responsible sups
      with one of his girls,
Responsible boozes all night.
He pinches his mistress,
        merry and sly,
"Here's my gift
      for the prettiest lass in the country!
Here's dough for perfume,
        and here, bye-the-bye,
for a stylish new pair of panties."
Such a rascal
      uses
        October's glow[150]

as a screen
                    to grab workingmen's money.
Our impoverished country
                    he milks to throw
his pelf
        at the feet of his Sonya.
I suppose
        I could give a White Guard my hand,[151]
squeeze it without revulsion:
I'd only grin at him—
                    "You and your band,
you got it
        during the Revolution! "
When a guy pinches bread,
                    you don't cry for penalty,
even a murderer
            can be condoned—
maybe he's ill
            and the gloom of insanity
hovers
        under his dome?
But if a brute
            who's been bribed with a ruble,
touches my palm
            with his own,
washing my hand,
            with a brick I'll scurb off
all the polluted skin
            to the bone.
Our legs still limping
                after our fight,
for us,
        patched,
            half-famished,
                    like beggarly tribes,
More fearful than any foe or blight
is
    the taker of bribes.
Our Party
        has issued its slogan steely,
arrived at
        after no little starving!
Away with
        every parasite,
                stealing
into our ranks and purses
                    to pinch our farthings.
We're building
            to grow to gigantic size—
but these
        settle down around cashiers.

Our Party,
        our workers
                will cauterize
with red-hot iron
                this growth mendacious!

(1926)

A MESSAGE TO PROLETARIAN POETS*

*Translated by
Peter Tempest*

Comrades,
        please,
                dropping all airs
                        and pretences,
I'd like as your sensitive,
                far from stupid
senior,
        to talk with you,
                Comrade Bezymensky,
Comrade Svetlov
        and Comrade Utkin.[152]
We argue hotly,
        our throats need tinning,
we're restless
        and breathless
                from triumphs on stage,
so I put it to you, comrades,
                a sound proposition!
A convivial
        dinner-party
                let's arrange!
With flowery compliments
                the floor we'll carpet,
scrub dirty looks clean
                without more ado;
put the laurels
        dispensed
                by Lunacharsky
in the stockpot
        to flavour
                our common stew.
Let's agree
        we are all
                right
                        each in his way.
Each sings
        with his own voice
                in one chorus!

Let's carve
                our common roast chicken of fame
and make sure
                every one
                                gets a portion.
Let's give up
                backbiting
                                and squabble no more
but start
                conversing
                                in a civilized way.
So that,
                when comrades
                                give me the floor,
I'll take it,
                rise to my feet and say:
"I may seem
                a fat-arsed
                                academician,
the sole
                high priest
                                of inscrutable verses.
But really
                for just one thing
                                I'm wishing—
to see more poets
                writing well
                                and diversely.
Many
                go job-hunting,
                                their sole care is
to get
                a posh title,
                                a high position:
"We are the only ones,
                                we proletarians..."
So what am I then?
                                A currency swindler?
Basically
                I'm
                a workman, brothers.
High-flown
                philosophy
                                bores me so.
I roll my sleeves up—
                                for work?
                                                for struggle?
That's what you fancy?
                                Well then, let's go!
We've
                an enormous task
                                before us—

poetry is needed
              by everybody.
So let us labour,
              not sparing our forces,
for a greater quantity
              of better quality.
The Commune's
              my yardstick
                      for gauging verse,
the reason
          the Commune
                  has won my heart is
the Commune's
          the highest point
                  on Earth,
the Commune's
          the greatest depth
                  we've charted.
In poetry
          there are no
                  friends
                      or relations,
with patronage
          you cannot weave   .
                      your rhymes.
It isn't our job
          to dish out
                  decorations,
abusive labels
          let's cast aside.
It's my belief—
          and I speak
                  without arrogance,
not boasting
          it's a novel idea
                  I've found—
the Commune's
          a place
                  where officials will vanish,
a place where
          song and verse
                  will abound.
We hear
          a few decent rhymes—
                      and on an aspiring
pigmy
          the title of "genius" falls.
One such fellow
          gets called
                  "the red Byron",

another—
      "the Reddest Heine of all".
One thing I dread
          in myself and in you
is shallowness of spirit,
             lest we end up giving
communist status
          to the platitudes
the gallery loves,
          and to barnyard jingles.
We're one in spirit,
          I don't need to tell you.
There's nothing divides us
          along the heart line.
If
   you're not with me,
          if we
          don't stand together
we might as well
          throw in the towel,
             resign!
And if I
      brandish my pen
          as I argue,
and throw
      in your face
          a rebuke or two,
it's a right I've won,
          as they say,
          the hard way,
by fashioning
      many more rhymes
          than you.
Comrades,
      let's banish
          such mercantile thoughts as
"My verse is
      my stall in the market place! "
All I have written
      is all yours also—
my rhymes
      and themes,
          my diction,
          my bass!
What's more capricious
      and fragile
          than fame?
Can I take it
      into my grave
          when I'm buried?
I don't give a farthing, friends,
          don't give a damn

for money,
   or glory,
     or similar rubbish.
Why should we
   carve up
     poetical sway?
Let's heap up
   words
    both caressing and withering
and
 without envy
   or snobbery
     lay
these word-bricks of ours
    in the Commune we're building.
Comrades,
   let's march all in step
     together.
We don't want to hear
   egg-heads'
     tiresome tirades!
If you must swear—
   look, there are foes in plenty
on the other side
   of the Red barricades.

(1926)

A FACTORY OF BUREAUCRATS*

*Translated by
Dorian Rottenberg*

He was sent here
   to put things in order.
In his pocket—
   a pen and a party card.
Middle-aged,
   middle-weight,
    middling clever,
his mind full of plans,
   grim resolve in his heart.
He goes
 and directs
   with forceful gestures.
It looks,
  a new era's in close perspective.
Himself
  pokes his nose
    into every question,

Glares at each,
                    from messenger to director.
With attention for details,
                    however small,
his zealous bosom glows,
but words
            bounce off
                    like balls from a wall
from his official brows.
What's that to the office?
                    Just listens, damnation!
though bright as the sun you may flare,
it stokes all your zeal
                    into applications,
letters
        and questionnaires.
Treat every paper
                    with just disgust!
If you let them
                    seize hold of your soul,
your brains
            that same day
                    will well nigh bust
with the paperwork
                    rigmarole.
They register everything
                    and like thread at the binders'
to report
            with their folders
                            appear:
"Will you please
                    sign your name here,
                            and here too, kindly,
and here too,
            and here too,
                    and here..."
The chief
            sticks to papers
                        like a forest tick,
initial zeal
            without trace
                    sunk in ink.
Yes,
    one's surroundings
                    make one's skin
                            very thick,
surroundings
            are a lousy thing.
He peers—
            paler than chalk his face—
through the official murk,

his sweat pours down,
                        his fountain-pen scrapes,
his hand gets numb,
                        yet again sets to work.
But,
        without end
                    in a white mass
                                    apace
grows
        the paperberg.
Whatever you like
                    he'll sign straight off—
                                        nope,
not giving a damn
                    about where, why or who.
His very own aunt
                    he'd appoint as Pope,
even sign his own death sentence,
                                    too.
His Party conscience's
                        weakening squeak
damped down daily
                    by paper loads,
he discovers the art of correspondence,
                                        so to speak,
licks his chops,
                plunges in
                            and with pleasure glows.
Where are resolve,
                    grand plans
                                and burning?
He summons his office
                        to hammer things home:
"Immediately find out
                        both name and surname!
Who dared send an envelope
                            with surname alone?"
And again
            flies his voice
                            in tiny barklets:
"Will proper procedure
                        ever begin?
You've written simply 'applied'—
                                here, mark it! —
and forgotten to write 'herein'! "
Having scribbled away
all through the day,
flooding Russia with papers
                            that no one needs,
in a car he'll stuff
his belly and off

to his villa
                in portly importance he speeds.
No more use from him
                        than milk from the devil
or from buckwheat porridge—
                        gold ore.
Only in vaults
                accounts rise level
with the ceiling,
                all ink-splotched,
                                whole tons and more.
Swarms of officials
                week in, week out
annul October's thunder;
                        on their bottoms
many,
        waggling them about,
even show
        pre-February
                eagle-bearing buttons.[153]
A poet,
        invariably kind and gallant,
to share my conclusion
                        I'm glad:
firstly,
        anybody with the proper talent
can turn
        into a bureaucrat.
Secondly,
        from feuilleton water
it's followed
                a thousand times or so:
a communist's no bird
                        and never ought to
acquire
        a tail of paper,
                        you know!
Thirdly,
        by the scruff he's got to be jerked
up
        from paper
                all dotted by flies,
so that straight-
                and crooked-signed paperwork
shouldn't hide communism
                        from his eyes!

(1926)

Translated by
Dorian Rottenberg

TO COMRADE NETTE—STEAMER
AND MAN[154]

Not in vain I start.
          No ghost-tale rubbish, reader.
Through the harbour's molten sunshine,
                        past the jetty
steams
      the very self
           of Comrade THEODORE
NETTE.
Yes, it's he;
        all in a hurry to arrive,
through those lifebuoy-saucer spectacles
                    he looks.
"Hullo, Nette!
        How I'm glad that you're alive
with the smoking life of funnels,
              ropes
                and hooks.
Pull up here!
        I hope it's not too shallow.
Tired,
    I fancy,
        boiling all the distance from Batum.
Once you were a man...
           Remember,
               dear old fellow,
the tea that on a train we would consume?
One eye cocked
        towards your red-sealed cargo,
nights on end,
        while others snored away
about old Romka Yakobson[155]
           you'd argue,
memorizing poems
        in your funny way.
Off you'd drop at dawn.
           Is that revolver there?
Better mind their business,
           if they're wise!
Could I think
        that only in a year
I should meet you
        in this cargo-steamer guise?
There's the moon come up.
          A stirring sight, I'll say!
Slashing space in two,
        astern she's looming;
as if, it seems,
        from that last battle in the passage way

your deathless hero-track
                were trailing,
                      blood-illumined.
Your print-and-paper communism's not believed so readily.
"Balloney, boy!
              It's true in books alone."
But things like these
              will show you communism bodily
transforming "fancies"
          all at once
                to flesh and bone.
We live under a pledge
              that grips in iron unity—
no crucifix will nail,
              no guns on earth will crush us—
all for humanity
            to live in one community,
not in a world all parcelled into Latvias
                  and Russias.
Blood
      runs in our veins,
              not lukewarm water.
Marching
       through revolver bark and blast,
when we die,
          it's to become immortal,
cast in steamers,
          verse
           and other things that last.
I could forge ahead
           through years and years,
but when life is done,
          there's nothing better
I should wish
         than meet the end
when my time nears
in the way
       that death was met
              by Comrade Nette.
Yalta
(15 July) 1926

PAPERWORK HABITS*

Translated by
Dorian Rottenberg

*English translation
©
Raduga Publishers 1985

Two months
      I've been spending
              in nature-rambles
to look at flowers,
          at starfire to look.

No such did I see.
                All Nature resembles
a telephone-book.
Throughout—
                on its rocks,
                            on the petrified jelly
of the Caucasus
                and Crimea,
                            its rock-faced mate,
on the walls of toilets,
                on the sky,
                        '   on the belly
of the horse of Emperor Peter the Great,
from road-dust
                to mountains
                            where storms arose
thundering,
                shaking their fiery tresses,
everywhere
                were excerpts
                            of verse and prose,
names,
        surnames
                and addresses.
"Here stopped Sonya and Vanya
                            Khailov.
The family ate and rested.
                        Hail, love! "
"Kolya and Zina
                joined fortunes here."
An arrow-pierced heart
                        shaped like a pear.
The slogan
                "Workers of the world, unite! " is
undersigned
                "Komsomol Pyotr Parulaitis".
"Monsieur Gog,
barber from Taganrog".
Up on a cypress
                centuries old,
the whole Russian alphabet
                        is enscrolled.
And this one's short,
                        yet it makes me eyesick,
inscribed
            an eagle eyrie
                        upon:
simple and sweet:
                "Isaac
Lebenson".

Let's not
            blame people
                        too much, goddamit.
Our folks can't do
                        without names and dates.
All their life's in paperwork,
                                it's become a habit:
they look at rocks too,
                        as if at mandates.
For such guys,
                watching at tea from a balcony
the sun
            going down in a clump of trees,
there's no sunset, no sunrise;
                                the sun is only
incoming,
            outgoing—
                        all officialese.
Damn!
            Put me in Rykov's place for an hour,[156]
I'd sign a decree
                of all-binding power:
"By the names
                left on trees and rocks
find
        the undersigned folks.
Into each bag—
a pail and rag,
then set them at large
and
        forward march!
Let all the undersigned
                            Zinas and Kolyas
erase with turpentine
                        all trace of their follies.
And—
        not to waste their energy—
                                give 'em petrol
to clean up the flanks
                        of Mount Ai-Petri.
And those
            who are so much inclined to sign
that again
            upon rocks they clamber,
such donkeys
                are to be banned for all time
from the use of their native grammar."
And then
            a flourish
                        beneath the decree:

Vladimir Mayakovsky,
                    that is, me.

Yalta, Simferopol, Gurzuf, Alupka
(1926)

THE HOOLIGAN*

Translated by
Dorian Rottenberg

Our Republic's in danger.
                    Into the door
breaks
        a beast
                never heard of before.
Ugly obscenities,
                raving,
                        it roars,
fists, knotted and hefty,
                        instead of paws.
Feet meant for kicking,
                no brains,
                        no sense—
that's the picture
                a hooligan presents.
A sailor-vest
        striped
                like a prison window
his beastly flesh
                is packed tightly into.
To give his baboon face
                a civilized look,
in shaving the fur off
                great pains he took.
Flakes of powder
                ("Swan-Down", mind you!);
a butterfly cravat
                from ear to ear, too.
Instead of a spirit
                (the gentry's invention)
Alcoholic spirits are all I can mention.
Feet stuck into shoes
                of the latest style,
swaying,
        he goes with a drunken smile.
At every stride
enemies hide.
Streetlamps—
                smash 'em! —
                        enemies sworn!

I'm in the dark—
                    let nothing burn!
Enemies—doors,
                    houses ahead.
Enemies—
          all who earn honest bread.
Enemies—libraries,
                    enemy—school.
Be silly everyone
                    if I'm a fool.
His belt swings
                    in his great big hands,
a cast-iron pound-weight
                              upon it hangs.
He swings it about
                    and the weight spins round.
Meet him—
          he'll knock you
                    down on the ground.
On a shady alleyway
                    shines the moon.
A girl walks alone,
                    eighteen soon.
"Damn pretty! "—
               he grabs her tight by the braid,
"Let's marry—
          without any registrar's aid."
No one'll hear her—
                    she yells in vain.
A stinking palm
               stops her mouth full of pain.
" 's none of our business—
                    not us being thrashed.
Run for it, boys,
                    before we're bashed! "
Behind the clouds
                    the scared moon backs
from the torn up bundle
                    of flesh and rags.
Then merriment reigns
                    in a bar not far.
Whistling,
          the lad swills beer in the bar.
By and by, though,
                    the lad gets caught.
The defence spares no words
                    when he's brought to court.
"Of course,
          the lad's a destructive force,
but who's to blame?
                    Surroundings, of course.

He's got so much strength,
                              it can't be curbed.
A true
        Russian hero,
                      in a word.
A hero of folklore.
                    Now,
                         if you please,
don't bother
             Russian heroes like these."
The defendant purses his lips,
                               purged of vice,
listening
          to a speech so nice.
He sits there,
               meeker and sweeter
than a sugar sheep,
                    damn creature.
And the judge—
                all clemency—
                              will declare
"4 months.
            That's time enough and to spare."
Now say,
         just four months for a beast!
                                        They've gone mad?
After all the harm
                    that's been done by the lad?
Get together,
              village and town,
                                and burn
with rage,
           let just indignation surge!
Let every farm
               and factory learn
of this latest
               and vilest scourge.
He
   whom no words will sober,
maybe he'll heed
                 a militiaman's sabre.
With resolve and discipline,
                             harden like steel,
workers' patrols,
                  for hoodlums to feel,
so that
        whenever a hooligan's grasped
all he could do
                would be sag and gasp.
When an invalid's arm
                      starts to rot

should we pity it?
                              Certainly not!
It's time
          the axe of the law
                              should chop off
rotten acts and words,
                              not just sneer and scoff!

(1926)

A CHAT IN ODESSA HARBOUR
BETWEEN S. S. *SOVIET DAGHESTAN*
AND *RED ABKHAZIA*

Translated by
Dorian Rottenberg

Clouds,
          come,
               lend the sunset west
                              canary-feathers!
Fall on sea and land,
                    black yoke of southern night!
Two ships at anchorage
                    begin a chat together:
one blinks—
          the other answers with a light.
What are they signalling?
                         I strain my forehead's furrow;
a red light flashes on
                    then fades
                              and turns to green.
Probably
          he wants a date tomorrow,
or perhaps
          just frets in jealous spleen?
Or perhaps
          he's asking,
                    "*Red Abkhazia,*
it's me,
          the gunboat
                    Soviet Daghestan.
Sulking all alone—
                what can be crazier?
Come here, baby,—
                let me hold your hand."
Silence.
        Then *Abkhazia* replies at last,
"Can't get on alone?
                    You'll have to learn.
'Cause I'm now in love
                    up to the mast

with the grey
      three-funnelled cruiser
                Komintern."
"All you women
      are just sluts
           and nothing else.
What's she see in him,
          that lumbering old braggart?"
And again he signals
      · with short yells:
"Hear me, someone,
      send us some tobacco!
It's dull here, on the searoads—
           dripping wet.
Fit to give one cramps
      and rust one's armour."
The whole world sleeps,
        the shimmering Black Sea shed—
a giant tear of blue—
      upon Odessa Harbour.

(1926)

PAPER HORRORS

(EXPERIENCED BY VLADIMIR MAYAKOVSKY)

*Translated by
Dorian Rottenberg*

If I held in
      my hands
        the planet's reins
I'd stop the earth for a minute:
          "Hark,
d'you hear
      pens scraping,
        fountain and plain,
as if
    the earth's teeth
        were grating in the dark?"
Men's pride,
      subside,
        be forever forgot!
To a dot
    humanity's future
        tapers.
Man
    is gradually
      becoming a blot
on the margins
      of enormously important papers.

Men are wedged like shadows
                        in domestic cubby-holes.
Ten square feet per nose—
                        yet for papers' glee—
whole castles of offices—
                        sprawl over tables
or lie back in safes
                        as content as can be.
Queues trail out
            for cloth
                        at a shop.
No galoshes for feet,
                        not a glove for your paw.
Yet for papers
            there's baskets,
                        a bumper crop,
and for "cases' " carcasses—
                        folders galore.
Rubles for travel—
            how many
                        have you?
Ever been in Madrid?
            I bet you
                        no!
Yet for papers,
            to enable them
                        to sail and travel
they're even erecting
            a new G. P. O.!
Thin as clips
            turn the legs
                        of the former strong.
Instructions oust brains—
                        no one feels the loss.
Men degrade into errand-boys
                        running along
in the service of paper
                        turned boss.
Papers burst
            from portfolios stodgy,
baring
      their white-totted hem;
soon people
            will crawl into portfolios
                        for lodgings,
as for flats—
            papers
                        will move into them.
I foresee in the future—
                        no fantasy of mine,

but a prophecy blared out
                              by paper trumpets:
papers
          shall sit at tables
                              and dine
and mannikins
                lie under the tables
                                    crumpled.
I'd unfurl
          a storm
                  of rioting banners—
tear papers with my teeth
                          and, indignant, yell:
"Every inch
          of useless paper,
                          proletarians,
hate like your enemy,
                    abhor like hell! "

(1927)

TO OUR YOUNG GENERATION*

Translated by
Dorian Rottenberg

On hundreds of stages
                      I've had to stand,
before thousands
                of keen young eyes.
How different
              the languages of their lands,
the clothes of their countless tribes!
Scarcely
          wiping the sweat off,
                                I
got through the narrow tunnel.
And,
      deafening with its whistled "Good-bye"
the express
            from Kursky Station
                                went running.
Factories,
          birches.
                    From forest to hut
speed pastures,
                their grasses waggling.
And pure,
          as if you were listening to MKHAT,[157]

comes Moscow's
                local vernacular.

From beyond horizons,
                    cut by woody patches,
a crowd of Ukrainian *mazanki*[158] advances.
Flowery,
          from under straw thatches
their walls peep,
               painted with diverse nuances.
Come with a sackful
               of most brilliant rhymes,
bust at the seams
            with talent,
the response will be
               condescending smiles
from Ukrainian laddies,
                nonchalant.
The expanses run,
            a gigantic plain
by the solar cook
            being fried.
Already Rostov
            approaches our train,
far beyond Kharkov
            we ride.
Fields—
         for millions of cereal tons
as if smoothed by a plane,
              lie flat.
In the ochre of wheatfields
              the silver Don
seems the tape
          on a Kuban hat.
We roar
        with our engine whistle
               till hoarse.
Now the Caucasus
           claims our attention.
Ranges like sugar-loafs
             tower on our course,
like firemen's helmets
            gleam in the sunshine.
Then we flew through canyons,
              with whistle subdued,
in the hoar of snows
           and fur hats.
Gripping their daggers,
             Ingushes stood.
Ossetins,[159]
       intent,
            in their saddles sat.
Mountain-tops—ice.

Their foot
   heat dries.
The sun pours iodine
     from the skies.
Tiflisians
   you'll recognize
      furlongs off:
they stroll at the hottest hour
in most stylish hats,
     shoes ne'er long-nosed enough,
real
  Parisians
    of ours.
Each learns ABC
    in his own special way,
figures also—
    his own has each.
Every third's from a nation
     whose name's hard to say,
with its own tongue
    kiddies to teach.
Once, dumping my things
     in a hotel hall,
I forgot
  where I'd spent the night.
Speaking in Russian,
    I asked a *Khokhol.*[160]
"Ne chuyu,"[161]
   the lad replied.
And when it comes
    to the sciences
you'd think they can't manage with Russian;
The academies
   of Kazan and Tiflis
use French for communication.
I too
  admire Paris
    by night and by day,
its boulevards—
    what could be better!
Yes,
  it's all very fine—
     Baudelaire, Mallarmé,
etc.,
  etc.,
   etc.!
Not for us, though,
   who marched
      through struggle-torn years,
through hardship,
    hazard
     and flame,

to grow our successors

       as boulevardiers,

as frenchified fobs,

      ours only by name.

Make use,

   all you

      who were tongueless and bare,

of Soviet freedom

      and breadth!

Seek for your root,

     your verb,

       try,

        dare,

dive into philology's depth.

Look boldly at life

      without blinkers and blinds,

clutch with eyes

     by learning obsessed,

all that's good

     in your own native climes

and all that's good in the rest.

But—

   no place

     for hatred's foul sneers.

No,

  don't sully red souls.

Young comrades,

      keep eyes on Moscow,

         train ears

to Russian consonants, vowels.

Why,

   were I a black

      whom old age hoars,

still,

  eager and uncomplaining,

I'd sit

  and learn Russian

      if only because

it

 was spoken

   by Lenin.

I know,

   when blood

     in the streets

       rushed in spate

in October's

    cannon-storms

      vicious—

it was here,

   in Moscow,

     we decided the fate

Of both Kievs
                    and Tiflises!
Moscow is not
                    an imperial lasso
lugging countries
                    in cattle-like manner.
Not as a Russian
                    I cherish it so,
but as a fighter
                    his banner.
I'm no *Katsáp*162
                    of super-mouth-girth.
There's three different sources
                              in me as to speech.
My grandads were Cossacks—
                              different each,
and myself
          I'm a Georgian by birth.
Three different blood-strains
                         wash past my cells,
so I take the right
                    to say let's
pack All-Union philistines
                         off to hell,
both your ones
          and *Russopets!* 163

(1927)

MY BEST POEM*

*Translated by
Dorian Rottenberg*

The audience
              pours questions
                         and barbed requests,
tries to nonplus me with notes,
                         but I'll show 'em!
"Comrade Mayakovsky,
                    please read your best
poem! "
Which poem
          should I honour
                    this time?
I think, fists propped on the desk.
Maybe I'll read them
                    this piece of rhyme,
or maybe
          that one
                    best?

While I shook up
                    my whole poetical archive,
and the hall sat in mute expectancy,
the secretary
            of the newspaper
                            Northern Worker
quietly whispered to me...
And I bellowed,
                quite off poetic tone,
louder than Jericho
                at its highest high,
"Comrades,
            the workers and troops of Canton
have occupied
            Shanghai! "164
As if
    they were mangling tin
                        in their palms,
the force of ovations
                    increased and increased.
Yaroslavl applauded,
                jerked out of its calm;
for ten, fifteen minutes
                    they wouldn't cease.
Over thousands of miles
                    the storm seemed to spread,
to all
    of Chamberlain's notes
                        in reply;
straight to China,
                and the steel shark-heads
of dreadnoughts
                turned away
                        from Shanghai.
I won't compare
                all poetic racket,
even the noisiest
                poetic fame
to this,
    the most simple newspaper fact,
if it wins
        Yaroslavl's applause and acclaim.
Oh, are there connections
                        stronger and greater
than solidarity
                linking workers so truly?
Applaud,
        Yaroslavl mill-operator,
your unknown
            yet dear brother,
                        the Chinese coolie!

(1927)

Translated by
Dorian Rottenberg

NOTHING NEW*

I opened
    with a quiet stir
the morning paper's
        eyes.
and felt the smell of gunpowder
from frontier lines
        arise.
No news for us,
      past twenty,
are storm and gale.
We've not much cause
        for gaiety,
yet none
    to wail.
History's water's
      turbulent.
In its expanses
      we
will cut
    through war's
        grim menace
like keels
    cut waves
        at sea.
(1927)

"BEYOND THE GRASP OF THE MASSES"*

Translated by
Peter Tempest

Between writer
    and reader
        stand men in the middle
and the intermediaries'
      taste
        is middling.
Among book reviewers,
      in editorial offices
there are thousands
      of just
        such
          mediocrities.
Wherever
    your thought gallops
      bright and bold
such a fellow
      will tell you
        with a sleepy stare:

"Now I'm
            a person
                        of a different mould.
There's a line of Nadson's,
                        I remember,
                                    where...
Short lines of verse
                        working men
                                    don't relish.
Aseyev too
            rails at
                        us middle men.
Full stops,
            like birthmarks,
                        verse embellish.
Don't omit
            punctuation
                        then.
If you wrote iambics,
                        Comrade Mayakovsky,
for each line
            I'd pay you
                        20 kopeks extra."
The fellow
            then tells you
                        a hoary tale or two,
wastes four hours
            of your precious time
                                    expressing
his views,
            and then says
                        of whatever you do:
"It's beyond the grasp
                        of workers and peasants."
Sensing his guilt,
            the author wilts humbly.
Yet the last time
            that influential critic
                                    saw
a peasant
            was out at his house
                        in the country
when he bought
            a leg of veal
                        before the Great War.
His acquaintance with workers
                        is even slighter—
two
            on a bridge
                        by chance he sighted

watching the river
        in spring
                overflowing
its banks
      and ice down the river going.
The critic
      gazed with an awestruck thrill upon
two representatives
           of ten million.
Nothing very special—
            with arms and chests,
people no different from anyone else!
That night
      he boasted,
            sipping his tea:
"If anyone
      knows the working class, it's me!
I
  read
     their minds
          though they said nothing there—
they sense no despondency,
           no despair.
Which authors
      do men of that class
            wish to read?
Nothing but Gogol,
        the classics indeed!
And peasants?
      It's exactly the same
          with them.
Out of town in the spring
         I remember when..."
Literary blathering like that,
         it so happens,
often
    takes the place
        of knowing the masses.
Thus pre-revolutionary patterns
         survive
in what artists by brush,
     pen
       and chisel contrive.
Thus out among the masses
       float
         wide and far
salon daydreams,
      roses,
        the twang of a guitar.
I beg you,
     intimidated writers—
        be mature

and stop
            lisping charity verse
                        for the poor.
The class
            that's playing a leading part
has no worse a grasp than you have
                        of art.
Spread
            the best of culture
                        among the masses,
the same as for everyone,
                        the quintessence.
Good books
            are needed
                        and within the grasp of
you
      and me,
            and workers
                        and peasants!

(1927)

YEKATERINBURG-SVERDLOVSK[165]

Translated by
Dorian Rottenberg

Out
      of the dazzle
                  and glare of snow
from a tangle of twigs
                  that stuns and bewilders
emerges,
            unseen a minute ago,
Sverdlovsk,
            new city of fighters and builders.
Yekaterinburg
            scooped out
                        all its bowels for carats,
hacking
            into icy bedrock and ore
for gems
            to glitter
                  on high-born parrots
like Kate the Great,[166]
                  the imperial whore.
They split
            their spines
in the entrails
            of mines,

till,
    into the streets
        by October hurled
they rose
    in the mightiest of upheavals
and went and packed off
        Catherine's eagles
and Catherine's heir
        to another world.
But then
    through the city
        war came thundering;
Kolchak and Gaida,[167]
        horde upon horde
had their go
    at whipping and plundering,
playing havoc
    with bullet and sword.
Gone
    are these days
        of banners and fires
leaving a scar
    for all times to remember:
the crimson flag
    in the Sverdlovsk skies
smouldering
    like an undying ember.
Beneath,
    from expanses
        ablaze with snow
the buildings of new-born Sverdlovsk grow,
electric lights
    make the night sky gay,
up
  into heaven
    the housetops burrow,
of a height
    that a skyscraper gladly would borrow,
while alongside
    the remnants of hell loom grey,
as if
  this city
    had no TODAY,
but only
    YESTERDAY
        and TOMORROW.
'Twixt office and bank
    in a sleigh you whizz
sweeping a mainstreet
    pygmied by none,

when WHOAH!
                    What conjuring trick is this? —
The mainstreet jolts to a halt in its run.
The stars' tobacco-dust
                    lies, wide-scattered
from the celestial pouch
                    in the black of night.
Smoking,
          the furnace-lungs heave and clatter,
and chimneys like pipes
                    in the river glow bright.

This city
          has no traditions hallowed,
no palaces,
          avenues,
                    fountains refined.
Before our eyes
          it is being alloyed
of the Urals,
          of vigour
                    and hard work combined.

(1928)

HOW FOUNDRYMAN IVAN KOZYREV
MOVED INTO HIS NEW FLAT*

Translated by
Dorian Rottenberg

I'm a proletarian.
                    No need for expounding.
As my mother bore me,
                    I used to live.
And here
          I'm given a flat
                    by my foundry
workers'
          housing co-operative.
Roomy—
          lumme!
                    Lumme—
                              its height!
Ventilated,
          heated
                    and lighted.
Yet
     it was this
          that most held my sight,

made me
          most delighted—
it's more divine
               than the promised land,
whiter
     than the moon
                    on its heavenly path.
It—
    but no words suit a thing so grand—
it's
    the bath!
From one tap
            water
                 runs freezing cold,
from the other—
                too hot to hold.
The cold water's good
                     to cool your poll,
the hot—
        to wash sweat
                     from your pores.
The right tap
             bears the inscription
                               "COLD",
the left one—
             "HOT" of course.
You come home
             fagged out,
                         just fit to hang.
Neither cabbage-soup gladdens
                             nor tea a-boiling.
But dive in,
            and you burst out laughing,
                                       old man,
all this tickling,
                  trickling,
                            enjoying.
As if
     · you'd come
                  to pay Socialism a visit—
it catches your breath,
                       it pleases you so.
Hang up your pants
                  and blouse
                            and get busy:
grab soap in your paw
                     and—splash—
                                 in you go!
You sit down
            and wash,
                     it seems,
                              for ages.

In short,
            you sit
                        as long as you wish.
As if you were in the Volga
                        bathing,
except that there aren't
                        no boats, no fish.
Though the dirt on your skin
                        may be thick and dark,
collected since years ago,
it comes off,
            bloody old stuff,
                        like bark,
whether it likes to
                        or no.
You sit,
            all steaming,
                        with heat all red.
And here—
            turn the handle round—
and like rain
            the shower
                        comes down on your head
from a hole-riddled
                        iron cloud.
My dear,
            how sweet
                        that shower appears,
all blues,
            all gloom
                        washed away
                                    with its aid.
It strokes your hair,
                        it ruffles your ears
and runs down the groove
                        'twixt your shoulder blades.
You wipe the water
                        from your skin,
                                    soaking wet,
with a towel
            as shaggy
                        as a bear laid flat.
So your soles should keep dry,
                        the floor is spread—
goddam my eyes—
                        with a corkwood mat.
Having looked yourself over
                        in a mirror,
                                    put on
a shirt
            as fresh-smelling
                        as any flowers.

It's a proper thing,
                    when all's said and done,
this Soviet power
                    of ours!

Sverdlovsk
28 January 1928

OFFICE-BUGS*

Translated by
Dorian Rottenberg

New young folk
                    appear of late
perfectly well-bred
                    and dressed.
Golden badges
                    decorate
every
        corresponding breast.
Partcom gnats
            from MKK[168]
on these lads
                their stings won't use:
duly noted,
            duly paid
are T. U.,
        Part.
                    and other dues.
Honest as a bullock,
                        he
rooted to his armchair
                        grows
and cannot
            and will not see
farther
        than his own young nose.
Communism exams
                    once past,
memorizing
            every *ism*,
he decides
        he's done at last
with all thought of Communism.
Why look farther
                than another?
Sit and wait for circulars!
Think?
        Why should we, buddies,
                            bother

if our leaders think for us?
Petty businesses
                    like blinkers
pulling over
              both his eyes,
he performs his job
                    un-thinking,
narrow,
         tranquil,
                    donkey-wise.
These days
         with embezzlers,
                              what-d'ye-pleasers
and diverse flatterers
                    running rife
for such folks
              are Socialism
implemented
              in real life.
To Communism
              still far-off gleaming
with such hacks
              we'll never come—
specially created
              seeming
for obtuse officialdom.
With gold badges
              all aglitter,
proudly sticking out their breasts,
quietly go
              such nice young critters,
well-adapted
              and well-dressed.
In the backwoods
                    of stagnation
such young folks
                    forever park,
while on the wall,
                    for decoration,
Karly-Marly's beard
                    shows dark.
What to do with lads like these,
honestly officialese?
YCL—er!
              Living in your great time,
October's
         ozone
                    breathing,
remember,
         each day
                    is a step
                              in the climb

to the goal
              that we're set
                      on achieving!
Not ours
          are those
                  who new paths won't pave,
forever
        stuck in Time's rear.
To be a Communist
                  means to be brave,
to think,
          to desire,
                    to dare.
What we have
              is still far
                      from a paradise,
with this philistine
                    silt and mould.
Working,
        don't get stuck in trifles.
                                  Your eyes
on our gigantic target
                      hold!

(1928)

THE COWARD*

Translated by
Dorian Rottenberg

Moderately
          fair-haired
                    or dark,
tastes undemonstrable,
                      eyes meekly lowered,
shadow-like,
            sideways—
                    Look out! Hark! —
over this country
                  by bravery marked
crawl
      reptilian
              cowards.
For a coward
            every senior's
                          an ace.
Even from his kin
a coward
        buries
              his eyes and face

in his collar
                pulled up
                        on his chin.
Both his eyes
              to papers soldered,
like compasses
                both legs fold.
Oh,
    to hide
          behind an order,
in official script
                be rolled!
'Twould be futile
                to try and conjecture
is he human
            or fish,
                live being
                        or fossil?
Won't even venture
                an extra interjection;
as for seal
          or signature—
                      quite impossible!
Only not to be elected,
never
      be responsible!
No less
        than a metre long
                        his ear,
after his seniors
                he'll follow,
their
      most gloried opinions
                        to hear,
and to tell them
                the same
                        tomorrow.
And if
      his senior
              changes his mind
he picks up
          the new opinions
                        to use 'em.
Opinions
        are things
                you can always find—
nothing to fear
              if you lose 'em.
Rob
    or kill someone
                  under his nose—
he'll never listen
                to ah's or oh's.

None of his business,
    he'll say,
       that's all!
He's not the Grand Dumb,
       but won't blab like a mortar!
Yes,
  his mouth is filled up with water
very much
    like a washing-bowl.
Lined, bark-like,
     with papers,
        front and back,
"Me take decisions?
     Let others take 'em.
What if they fail
     and I get the sack?"
So he meditates, unshaken.
All day long
    he's subtly tying
ties
  for the most odd of weddings:
linking up
   a lamb and lion,
cats and mice
     together blending.
With all sorts of fears
      his heart's piled high;
he shivers
   and quivers
      all day through,
afraid of buses
    and RKI,[169]
his chief,
   his wife,
      the 'flu,
the *mestkom*,[170]
     the *domkom*,[171]
        folks begging for loans,
graveyards,
    militiamen,
      forests,
dogs,
   gossips,
     winter,
      being alone,
and show-trials,
     first and foremost.
He'll shiver all day
     and to bed he'll go
to shiver again
    all night.

Comrade,
              why are you shivering so?
Your health doesn't seem
                        all right!
Is it the ague
              or some other pain?
Revolutionaries
              shouldn't be gutless as porridge!
Courage,
         courage
                 and once again
courage!

(1928)

LINES NOT ON BIG
              BUT PETTY TRASH.
LET BARB-TONGUED RHYMES
                        THIS SPECIES LASH! *

Translated by
Dorian Rottenberg

Everyone knows
              that I've sung about trash
at the dawn
         of my days.
But trash won't die off.
                        Let my poem's flash
new trash
         from the earth
                        erase.
Philistines
         crawl into every chink.
They've refurbished
              the life
                        meant for demolition.
Today such humans
              readjust—
                        just think! —
into sitting asses—
              a queer new edition.
We're in doldrums today.
                        Today won't arise
trash with
         features
                 genuine and typical.
Today
         such folks
                 diminish in size,

trivial,
>> petty,
>>>> little—
>>>>> like spittle.
He's survived the Revolution,
>>>>> lived until NEP
and goes on adjusting,
>>>> as we move ahead.
He's cunning—
>>> nothing surprising,
>>>>>> yep,
for even a pin
>>> has a head!
Somewhere
>>> bullets
>>>> tear banners' silk.
Starving China
>>>> arises in riot,
yet he won't give a damn,
>>>>> he and his ilk,
feeling warm
>>>> and snug,
>>>>> well pleased with his diet.
Very quietly
>>>> the border's erased
between real trash
>>>> and the philistine race.
Canaries
>>> have gone to rest
>>>>> on the dump;
less birds—
>>>> less unneeded expenses.
With industrialization
>>>>> grammophones come,
canary-coloured
>>>> lamp-shades and dresses.
He's fixed up
>>>> the cosiest little alcove
>>>>> for his bed.
Now try and calm him,
>>>> an uncultured pest.
He takes
>>>> the most interesting book to be read—
a savings-book—
>>>>> and leafs through its pages with zest.
The kindliest
>>>> family-man,
>>>>> so he will reason,
gloating
>>>> and counting over his pelf:

"Almighty,
                save me from prison,
and from IWH[172]
                I'll save me myself! "
Against this swollen,
                slick domesticity
how long must poets
                keep bruising their tongues?
Inventors,
                give us a universal pesticide
bed-bugs
                and philistines
                                killing at once!

(1928)

CRIMEA*

*Translated by
Dorian Rottenberg*

It's simply silly
                to call it "Red Nice".
"All-Union Resort"–
                is there anything drearier?
Crimea–
        there's nothing
                        nearly so nice!
Nothing's comparable
                with our Crimea!
Flowers
        above,   ,
                alongside
                        and under;
vines
        stuck up
                onto poles–
                        a real wonder!
With wine and flowers
                you're drunk in Oreanda;
it's all flowers and wine
                in Massandra!
The air is yellow,
                yellow–the sand.
All comparison's
                bound to fail.
The sun
        burns your skin
                        like a cattle-brand
put to a horse
                near its tail.

Nature
          squanders her flowers
                              lavishly
for the sun—
              that big goldy-head.
And all of it
              pleased
                        just one tsar once
                                        slavishly!
Just funny—
              when all's done and said.
And now
          the wind
                    strokes the flower-band,
ruffles
        the flags' red flame.
Dozens of sanatoriums stand,
bearing Lenin's,
                  Dzerzhinsky's,
                                October's name.
Our worker-lads
                are cheery and glad,
in shorts-wearers' ranks
                          enlisting.
Grapes are already
                    maturing like mad,
their vine-mustachios
                        twisting.
The city's
            joyous—
with growth so lusty
soon—
        boyo! —
they'll pile us
                with clusters.
Take any park—
                they're full,
                              one and all.
Look into the shadow
                      of lane and alley:
sanatorians
            keep busy
                        with volleyball
or simply
          shilly-shally.
A rifle pounds
                at a target board;
they learn
            to knock Chamberlain down
                                    at a stroke.

Aim better!
                    The head of a British lord
is harder
                than any iron or oak!
Others
        on beaches
                        settle down,
bronzing their bellies
                        in suitable poses.
Still others
                go gulping yogurt down,
or smelling
                all sorts of roses.
An earthquake
                    tore up the road here,
                                    shattering
huts
        built up
                near the very sky.
It roared like Vesuvius,
                        old Ai-Petri.
Ay, Petri!
            Ay-ay-ay!
But while
            I'm doing my job
                            as a poet,
to quench wild Nature
                        and finally conquer it,.
workers
        put on the brute—
                        they'll show it! —
a new strait-waistcoat
                    of reinforced concrete.

Alupka
25 July 1928

YOUTH'S SECRET*

Translated by
Peter Tempest

Not those
can be called "the youth"
who sprawling
                    in meadows, in boats
to squealing
                and shouts uncouth

pour
        vodka
            down their throats

Mayakovsky among Red
Armymen at a book bazaar.
June 1929

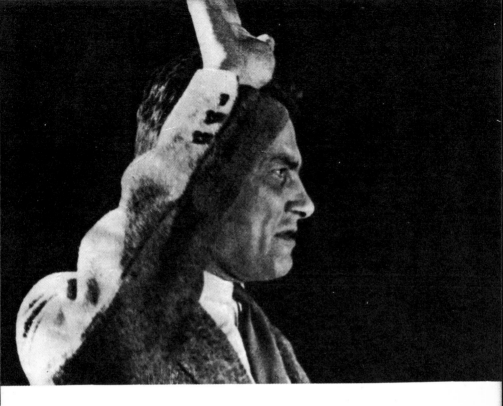

Mayakovsky. From a 1929
newsreel

Mayakovsky. 1929. Photo by
A. Temerin

Mayakovsky among Ukrainian
delegates at a writers' conference. 1924. Photo by M.
Ozersky

Poster announcing Mayakovsky's exhibition "20 Years of
Work". 1930

Mayakovsky with a young
audience at the exhibition
"20 Years of Work". February
1930

Mayakovsky among a group
of writers at the exhibition
"20 Years of Work". 1930.
Photo by L. Leonidov

Not those
          can be called "the youth"
who
     fouling spring nights with their fags
go sweeping,
               as with a broom,
the boulevards
               with flared bags.
Not those
          can be called "the youth"
who squander
               on love affairs
their first glow of life,
                    the new
vigour
     their bloodstream bears.
No,
   youth
          isn't made of such stuff.
To be eighteen
               just isn't
                    enough.
The youth
          are those who, when they see
the fighting line thinning,
                    assert
on behalf
          of all children:
                    "We
shall refashion life
               on Earth! "
The title
          of youth
                    is a favour
given
     members of the K. I. M.,[173]
given
     those who strive
                    so labour
be light
          and a joy to all men!

(1928)

THE PILLAR*

Translated by
Dorian Rottenberg

Comrade Popov's
        all but fresh from the plough,
all but fresh from the lathe,
          be it known.
He's even
      a party-member,
          but now
scared,
      he intones
          in a grumbling tone.
"Open
      the paper—
          it's all criticism,
no difference—
          foe or friend.
They snap at—
          who do you think?
               Gee whiz!
What names!
          Makes one's hair stand on end!
Subversion,
      I call it,
          sheer sabotage.
Criticism
      should be applied
          with caution,
and here—
      they're sparing
          neither prestige
nor title,
      nor office,
          nor hopes for promotion.
Criticism
      from below
          is a bane.
From the top—
      it's medicine,
          yes!
Can we let everyone,
          if we're sane,
criticize
      everyone else?
We wash our foul linen,
          we lay it on hot!
In papers
      we make it an issue.
S'pose I *am* mistaken?
          So what?

*English translation
©
Raduga Publishers 1985

Here,
            at my work,
                        there's a special commission!
Can't it be done
                        without rocking pillars,
among our own ilk—
                        our fellow-brethren?
Can't they simply summon
                        and simply tell us,
'Comrade Popov,
                carry on...
                        ...less heftier'?
It gets down to one's guts!
                        It makes you vomit,
being laid on so thick.
Comrades,
            but this is subversion,
                        dammit!
Cuts the roots of the state
                        to the quick!
Who's being criticized?"
                        worked up, he'll yelp
over the intercom.
"Yesterday Ivanov,
                today myself—
tomorrow
            it'll be
                Sovnarkom! "174
Comrade Popov,
                please shut up your trap.
This tattle about subversion's
                        all crap.
We call on all
            to slash out with the truth,
criticize filth,
                not half-way,
                        but full-length!
And that will be
                the best possible proof
of our purity
                and our strength.
(1928)

THE TOADY*

*Translated by
Dorian Rottenberg*

*English translation
          ©
Raduga Publishers 1985

People
            of this sort
                        are quiet
and as shapeless
                        as meat-jelly.

Very many
       of their like
make careers today,
           folks tell me.
Rich
     in neither flesh nor wit,
Pyotr Ivanovich Boldashkin
wears a head
       much better fit
to become a cane-knob,
          dash it!
Now this vegetable basks
in his tender boss's
        sunshine.
What's the secret,
        you may ask,
of such fatherly
        attention?
Putting on
       both weight and gloss,
he is getting on
       in life,
all because
       he treats his boss
gentler
    than a lawful wife.
With a smile
       and with a bow,
licking finger,
       licking toe,
like a milk-calf
      licks a cow,
like a piglet
     licks a sow.
And his tongue?
        Miles long, suave,
sticking out
      to reach the chief,
all in lather—
      he can shave
without soap—
      it's past belief!
Once he's started,
      he will praise
all that comes
      into his mind:
your catarrh,
     your rank,
        your age,
or a wart
    on your behind.

He's promoted—
                    even set
as a model of behaviour.
Wait a while,
                    and he will get
hold of power—become our Saviour!
Once his hand
                    is on the helm,
as it could have been expected,
he will drool:
                    "Remember well:
authority
                    must be respected! "
We look on,
                    in gloom remarking
how from toadyish
                    hypocrisy
grows
        a true-blue hierarchy,
in profanation of democracy.

Oh,
        to take a great big besom
and sweep all
                    who've given in—
toadies
            and pro-toadyism—
into one big garbage bin!

(1928)

THE GOSSIP*

*Translated by
Dorian Rottenberg*

Pyotr Ivanovich Sorokin,[175]
to all feelings
                    cold as ice,
neither drinking wine
                            nor smoking,
hasn't got
            a single vice.
One grand passion
                    like a river
inundates his heart
                        alone:
he adores
            like some queer earring
to hang on the telephone.
Stuffed with gossip—
                        choicest dainties—

tripping
　　　like a goat
　　　　　　he goes
to the first
　　　recalled
　　　　　　acquaintance
to divulge
　　　the news he knows.
Choking,
　　　wheezing
　　　　　　from emotion,
covering
　　　no meagre
　　　　　　distance,
he will add
　　　a good proportion
of the nicest,
　　　spiciest details.
"Well,"
　　　he'll start,
　　　　　　on shaking hands,
"it's a funny story,
　　　　　　very.
Alexandr
　　　Petrovich
　　　　　　Pants
lives with his own secretary.
And Ivan Ivanych Shishkin,
our Trust's leading engineer,
a year ago
　　　went on a mission.
Now
　　　his home-coming
　　　　　　is near.
As for *her*,
　　　excuse me,
　　　　　　　soon
she's expecting..!
　　　　　　What a scream!
By the way,
　　　friends,
　　　　　　all the town
says
　　　that one night, in a dream..."
Cupped palms
　　　hide his lips, white-scared;
mister's face gets sharper,
　　　　　　paler:
"The Gubcommittee[176] has declared
an ultimatum
　　　to Australia! "

Dishing out
        some other items
with this queer announcement
                grouped,
promptly he reports,
          the blighter,
what his neighbours
          had for soup,
who ate what
        for lunch and dinner,
has Miss X
      another lover,
and whose purse
          is getting thinner,
buying gifts
      for Ivanova.
If we happen
        to ask such a bird
what his greatest wish is,
            he sighs,
what he wishes
          is that all the world
would become
        one keyhole
              of giant size.
So that
      squeezing into that keyhole
                one third
of his bulk,
       including his head,
he could go peeping,
          inspired and stirred
into others'
       affairs and beds.

(1928)

TASTES MAY DIFFER

Translated by
Dorian Rottenberg

The horse
        saw the camel
             and laughed herself hoarse.
"Such
      a tremendous
          freak of a horse! "
The camel rejoined:
         "You—a horse?
              Not nearly!

You're an underdeveloped camel,
                              merely."
And only God,
              omniscient indeed,
knew they were mammals
                    of different breed.

(1928)

A LETTER FROM PARIS TO COMRADE KOSTROV[177]
ON THE ESSENCE AND MEANING OF LOVE

Translated by
Dorian Rottenberg

Comrade Kostrov,
                I'm sure you won't mind—
I know,
        generosity's one of your merits—
if part of the lines
                    for Paris assigned
I'll squander
              on petty lyrics.
Imagine:
          a beauty
                    enters a hall,
framed
        in necklace and furs,
and I
      says to her
                  with no preface at all
these very selfsame words:
I've
    just come
              from Russia, comrade.
In my country
              I'm a figure.
I've seen women
                far more comely,
women
      prettier
                and slimmer.
Girls   .
      go crazy
                over poets,
and I'm
        vociferous
                  and smart.
Come along!
            Just watch me do it.
Snub me?
        No one's got the heart.

You won't catch me
                    double-dealing,
dabbling
        in petty lust.
Deep down in my heart's
                    that feeling,
carry it through life
                    or bust!
I'll not measure
            love by weddings.
Leave me, would you?
                    Very well.
I don't give a damn,
                    I've said it,
for your bleeding wedding bells.
So, my girl,
            don't let's be dainty.
Let's not joke,
            Almighty God!
Mademoiselle,
            I'm long past twenty—
better call it thirty odd.
Love doesn't mean
                    just eternal unrest,
not the way
            one can burn and flare.
It's that
        which heaves
                    under mountain-breasts,
behind
        the jungle of hair.
To love means to rush out
                    into the yard
and right until ravening night
with a flashing axe
                    to chop faggots hard
in a fireworks
            of manly might.
To love
        is to break
                    from insomnia-torn sheets,
with jealousy of Copernicus
                    swallowing saliva;
him,
        not the husband
                    of Mrs. Sugar-and-Sweets
regarding
            as your most deadly rival.
Love
        for us
            isn't Eden and so on.

Love
          for us
                    booms that once again
our heart's
          too-long-cooling engine
                              will go on
working
          against
                    all odds
                              and pain.
You've severed
          with Moscow
                    every thread,
it's years
          since you
                    and it came to part.
Then how shall I hammer
                    into your head
the gist
          of that state of heart?
Lights cover the earth
                    right up the sky.
The sky's full of stars—
                    go, count the lot.
If I wasn't
          already a poet
                    I
would turn astronomer,
                    honest to God!
A hubbub fills
          both alley and square.
The traffic
          speeds past
                    like mad,
while I
          go sauntering
                    here and there
and jot down rhymes
                    in a pad.
The cars
          that race
                    along the street
won't knock me down
                    by chance.
They understand,
                    and so take heed:
the bloke's
          in a lyric trance.
A vortex of images,
                    ideas,
                              and visions

the sizzling city
                    brings.
Why,
        even a bear
                    in such conditions
would grow
            a pair of wings.
And then
            out of one of the third-rate bars
after stewing
                inside
                    for a time
a word
        zooms upward
                    straight to the stars
like a comet,
            all ashine,
its tail stretched out
                    over half the skies,
its plumes—
            the heavens' highlight,
for lovers to sit
                and feast their eyes
while smelling
                their arbour's
                        lilac;
to rouse
        and lead
                and enthuse
                        and uphold 'em,
those
    whose spirit is wavering,
to saw off enemies' heads
                    from their shoulders
with a glittering
                long-bladed
                        sabre.
I'll stand
        till the very last beat in my breast
as if
    on a rendezvous,
and listen
        to love
                booming on in its nest,
simple,
        human
            and true.
Sea-tide,
        hurricane,
                tempest
                    and flame

rumble inside me
and swell!
Who'd take such a pet
to own and tame?
You would?
Very well!

(1928)

A LETTER TO TATYANA YAKOVLEVA*178

*Translated by
Peter Tempest*

In each tremor
of those I cherish,
in each kiss
their lips bestow
the red
hue
of my republics
must
no less
eagerly
glow.
Parisian love
I don't relish:
dress a bitch
in a silken gown,
I'll stretch, yawn
and say:
"Hold steady! "
to rampaging passion's
hounds.
You alone match me
in stature,
brow to brow
come take your stand here!
And
about that
crucial evening
let us talk
like human beings.
Five hours
and ever since then
the pinewood
of people
is still,
hushed
is the teeming town.
I hear only
the whistling shrill
of trains Barcelona-bound.

Lightning flares
            in a black sky clearly,
thunder
      swears
          in the drama of heaven,
it isn't a storm
        but
          merely
the stirring of heaps
          of envy.
To foolish words
          give no weight.
Don't be scared away
          by this fever.
I shall bridle,
          yes, I shall tame
these inherited gentry
          feelings.
Passion measles
          pass with scabbiness
but pleasure
          shall never run dry.
For long to come
          simply and happily
I'll be talking aloud
          in rhyme.
Women,
      jealousy,
          tears...
          Enough of them! —
Like witches,
          their eyes red and swelling.
Not for myself,
        but...
          for the honour
of Soviet Russia I'm jealous.
I've seen
        the shoulder-patches of paupers
licked
      with a sigh
          by consumption.
It certainly wasn't
          our fault that
a hundred million
          suffered.
Kindness to them
         we
          now show.
Through sport
          you'll not straighten out many—
here in Moscow
          we too need you,

there's a shortage
                    of long-legged elegance.
It isn't for you
               who've gone stepping
through typhus
              and deep snowdrifts
to go offering
              your legs
                        after dinner
for oil kings
          here
               to kiss.
Don't screw up your eyes
                    and ponder so,
spoiling your arched brows' charms.
Come hither now,
              come to the crossroads
of my great
          and clumsy arms.
You don't want to?
                   Then stay and hibernate.
To old injuries
            we'll add a new.
All the same
          I shall take you
                          some day
on your own
          or with Paris too.
(1928)

CONVERSATION WITH COMRADE LENIN*

Translated by
Irina Zheleznova

Awhirl with events,
                    packed with jobs one too many,
the day slowly sinks
                 as the night shadows fall.
There are two in the room:
                          I
                            and Lenin—
a photograph
            on the whiteness of wall.
The stubble slides upward
                       above his lip
as his mouth
           jerks open in speech.
                                 The tense
creases of brow
              hold thought
                           in their grip,

immense brow
        matched by thought immense.
A forest of flags,
        raised-up hands thick as grass...
Thousands are marching
        beneath him...
            Transported,
alight with joy,
        I rise from my place,
eager to see him,
        hail him,
          report to him!
"Comrade Lenin,
        I report to you
(not a dictate of office,
        the heart's prompting alone)—
this hellish work
        that we're out to do
will be done
        and is already being done.
We give light to clothe
        the nude and the needy,
the quotas
        for coal
        and for iron
          fulfil.
But there is
        any amount
        of bleeding
muck
    and rubbish
        around us still.
Without you,
        there's many
        have got out of hand,
all the sparring
        and squabbling
        does one in.
There's scum
        in plenty
        hounding our land,
outside the borders
        and also
        within.
Try to
    count 'em
        and
        tab 'em—
        it's no go,
there's all kinds,
        and they're
        thick as nettles:

kulaks,
                red tapists,
                            and,
                                    down the row,
        drunkards,
                    sectarians,
                                lickspittles.
        They strut around
                        as proudly
                                    as peacocks,
        badges and fountain-pens
                            studding their chests.
        We'll lick the lot of 'em—
                            but
                                to lick 'em
        is no easy job
                    at the very best.
        On snow-covered lands
                            and stubbly fields,
        in smoky plants
                        and on factory sites,
        with you in our hearts,
                            Comrade Lenin,
                                        we build,
        we think,
                we breathe,
                            we live,
                                    and we fight! "

        Awhirl with events,
                        packed with jobs one too many,
        the day slowly sinks
                        as the night shadows fall.
        There are two in the room:
                            I
                            and Lenin—
        a photograph
                    on the whiteness of wall.

1929

TWO COMPETITIONS*

*Translated by
Dorian Rottenberg*

*English translation
©
Raduga Publishers 1985

I loop
        around Europe
                    in a railway tour
        through moonlit nights
                            and through smoky days.

God damn her!
                    She isn't no fool,
                                        for sure,
she's so clever,
                    comrades,
                                        you'd be amazed!
Here,
        on the endless threads
                                of go-getting
the beads of hours
                    are accustomed to setting;
each vies
            with the others
                                in grim consternation
in accord
            with the rules
                                of rationalization.
Frenchmen compete
                    with Englishmen ginger
who'll squeeze more out of workers,
                                        who's the stingier?
Parties compete
                    (British Labour—foremost)
in hoodwinking workers
                            through swindles enormous.
In police massacres
                        mauling and maiming,
vie local coppers (SD most worth naming).
Papers compete
                    at the top of their voices
whose lies about Russia
                            are the choicest.
"Peacemakers" compete
                        in the League of Nations
who'll lead in the arms-race,
                                who's most audacious.
"Neighbours",
                before they attempt an attack,
compete:
            whose mouth is most toothful and black.
Emigrées vie
                (lousy work, however):
who invents greater humbug
                            in crazy endeavour.
Poking the noses of guns at colonies,
chaining,
            squeezing,
                        gas-stench issuing,
proceeds
            Capitalist
competition.

The Bourgeois compete,
                    so why then do we
let drop
          our backwardness-slackened reins?
Speed on five-year plans—
                    let five be worth fifteen!
Let 'em see our muscles
                    bulging with veins!
In work and defence
                    come out competing!
To the young Republic's young builders—
                                   my greetings!

(1929)

ALL'S QUIET IN THE WEST*

*Translated by
Dorian Rottenberg*

Like a dove's conscience,
                    the asphalt's clear-spread.
The pavement's smooth
                    as a banker's bald pate
(after lorries
          have taken out the dead,
and the pavements are washed
                    from blood spilled in spate).
Bourgeois kiddies
          in gardens and yards
stroke their toy bears' velvet
                    to Nanny's tale
(after gas
          has been pumped
                    out of reservoirs,
and at midnight
          to Poland
                    tanks set trail).
Peacemakers
          gleam
                    with their top-hats' affluence
(each tongue, brandished, a sabre matches,
after rifles
          have been sent off
                    to the Afghans
and bombs
          despatched
                    to killer-basmaches[179]).
Dismounted hussars
                    in cafés
                    take up station.

Civilian-clothed,
                infantry
                        frolics, idle,
while feverish-crazy,
                beneath all this idyll
brass-hats
            proceed
                with war-preparations.
Crimson blood-drops
                in dash-line order
dripping,
            encircle the earth,
                        driven dizzy.
Assassins' bullets
                from round a corner
after their victims
                fly off,
                        whizzing.
Straight at the heart
                aims the deadly gun.
Those who command
                require but one thing:
quieting the ring-leaders
                one by one,
the rest
        like a sheep-flock
                    to slaughter to bring.
Today
        in small skirmishes
                        blood goes drizzling,
while tomorrow,
                poking tanks at the crowds,
war'll take relish
                in blood-baths grisly,
and lead and gas
                in bloody dung sizzling
hot,
        from armoured birds
                        will hit out.
Look ahead.
                in a none-too-distant year,
knocking bone against bone,
                            a hobby-horse shows,
and on it
        the yellowing skeleton of war,
death's scythe, steely-blue,
                        prepared to shower blows.
We—
        choice titbits
                for which cannon thirst,

we—
    a market for crutches
                  of every size,
we'll fill up the streets
                on August the First[180]
and nail
      our protest
           to the very skies.
Away
    with gunpowder-barrel politics!
Let no one
     at home
        scarily hide!
From the first Republic
        of peasants and workers
war's bayonet-tentacles
        push aside!
We clamour for peace,
        yet touch us—
           and promptly
we'll clench into regiments,
        grim and gaunt,
and massacre-mongers
        will see at the front line
one single
     rebellious
       workers' front!

(1929)

MY SOVIET PASSPORT

*Translated by
Dorian Rottenberg*

I'd rip out
    bureaucracy's guts,
        I would.
No reverence for mandates—
        good riddance!
Pack off to very hell
      for good
any old paper,
      but this one...
Past berths and compartments
        drawn out in a line
moves a customs official,
        most courteous-looking.
Folks hand in their passports
        and I hand in mine,
my crimson-jacketed
      bookling.

Some passports
              bring smiles
                        in a matter of instants.
Others
      are fit but to fie on.
Special deference
                is shown,
                          for instance
for those
         with the double-bed
                          British Leo.
Bowing non-stop,
                as if rocked by a ship,
eating their eyes
                into the "kind old uncles",
they take,
          as if they were taking a tip
the passports
           of lanky Yankees.
At Polish passports
                  they bulge out their eyes
in thick-skulled
              policemen's
                          donkeyness,
as if to say:
            what
                the devil are these
geographical
           novelties?
Without even turning
                   their cabbage-like heads,
hardly deigning
              to touch them,
they take,
          absent-minded,
                        the passports of Swedes
and all sorts
          of other Dutchmen.
But suddenly
           Mr. Officer's face
                          turns awry,
as if
     he has smelled disaster.
You've guessed it:
                  the officer's taken my
red-skinned hulk of a passport.
He handles it
            like a hedgehog
                          or bomb,
like a bee
          to be nipped
                      by the wings,

like a twisting rattlesnake
                        three yards long
with a hundred
                deadly stings.
The porter winks;
                to tell the truth,
he'd carry your luggage
                        free
                        all the way for you.
The gendarme
                looks questioningly
                        at the sleuth,
the sleuth looks back:
                        what to do with this wayfarer?
With what delight,
                by the gendarmes,
                        damn it,
I'd be flayed,
                crucified,
                        hanged
for the crime of holding
                        a sickled,
                                hammered
Soviet passport
                in my hand!
I'd rip out bureaucracy's guts,
                        I would.
No reverence for mandates—
                        good riddance!
Pack off to very hell
                for good
any old paper,
                but this one...
As
        the most valuable
                of certificates
I pull it
        from the pants
                where my documents are:
read it—
                envy me—
                        I'm a citizen
of the USSR!

1929

AMERICANS IN AMAZEMENT*

Translated by
Dorian Rottenberg

From its far-distant coast,
                    as if staring at spooks,
the USSR
         with its eye
                    devouring,
rising on tiptoe,
              America looks
through tortoise-shell specs,
                    unblinking, scowling.
What's that—
         a new breed
                    of the species Man,
there,
       on that far-off building-site piddling?
Fantasized
         with something they called
                              Five-Year Plan,
and now fulfil it,
              a year ahead of schedule?
Inapplicable here
              are American measures.
Unincited by dollars
                  and rubles, too,
at the very limit
              of human energy,
they work
         without holidays,
                    all the week through.
What sort of folk are they?
                    Maybe, iron?
What makes them tick,
              what's their driving principle?
They need no stick
              nor whiplash to drive 'em,
and yet they're clenched there
                    in steel-fisted discipline!
Misters,
       it's been your long-standing system
to buy with money
              a builder's zeal.
You won't understand,
                  overnourished misters,
why
    our communards' zest
                  is so real!
Bourgeois,
       stare at the Communist cohorts!

In trains,
                in planes,
                        in work of all kind
        your fleet-foot America,
                        famed for its know-how,
        we'll overtake
                        and leave way behind!

(1929)

HAPPY ME! *

Translated by
Dorian Rottenberg

Fellow-citizens,
                I've enormous
                        good news.
        Spread your faces
                in smiles
                        sympathetically.
        By any means
                I must share it with you,
        at any rate,
                poetically.
        I breathe
                like an elephant
                        today.
        My step
                is unusually light.
        Like a wonderful dream,
                        the night flew away,
        not a cough
                or a blob of spittle
                        all night.
        I'm getting pleasure
                in mammoth dozes.
        These autumn days
                have a bathhouse stink,
        yet for me,
                excuse me,
                        it's all just roses,
        and I go about
                and inhale them,
                        just think!
        Both ideas
                and rhymes
                        are most striking and nice.
        I'm sure,
                the editor's eyes'll pop out,
        I'm full of gumption,
                        end jobs in a trice,

as strong as a horse
                    or tractor,
                              no doubt.
My budget and digestion
                    are perfectly splendid,
improved
          and balanced—
                    just great!
A 100 per cent economy
                    on the main expenditure—
gains
      both in health
                and weight.
As if
      someone's piling
                    the most fantastic cake
on my tonguetip,
                bite after bite,
such a magical taste
                in my mouth's domain
has set in
          almost overnight.
My head
          has always been clean
                              externally.
Now it's clean
              within,
                    and, o boy! —
composes
          no less
                    than 10 pages diurnally,
enough
          to wipe the nose
                    of Tolstoy!
Women surround me,
                    each frock a hit,
all begging
          for autographs.
I'm definitely becoming
                    most famous as a wit,
wherever I turn up,
                    there's grins and laughs.
My face has become
                    far plumper and rosier,
forgotten
          are flu and bed.
Fellow-citizens,
                would you know the recipe?
Shall I say it,
          or leave it unsaid?

Fellow-citizens,
                    you're exhausted with waiting,
ready to start
                    reproaching and rebuking.
Don't be nervous.
                    Listen, maties:
Today
        I've given up
                    smoking.

(1929)

WE*

Translated by
Dorian Rottenberg

We're Edisons
            of unheard-of achievements,
                                energies,
                                    flights
                                        and lights.
But the main thing we cherish,
                        which never will be overshadowed,
is our Land of Soviets,
                    gaining daily in might,
our Soviet freedom,
                our Soviet sunshine,
                            our Soviet banner.
Dig deeper,
        soar higher,
leave others
        behind,
worker—
        inventor,
muster
    your mind!
Let our cabbage and carrots
                        in size be giants,
let our cattle and horses
                    make the rest look like ponies.
The masses' own flesh,
                the masses' own scions,
we're the Soviet countryside's
                        titan-Marconi's.
The struggle will spread
                into science soon,
classes
        versus classes.
Complete
        the edifice
                of the Commune,

employing
the wits
of the masses!
Let myriads
of power-plants
illumine the wilderness!
Compress
in collective brains
the brains of each woman and man,
to become titanic
never heard of yet Edisons
of our five-,
ten-,
fifty-year plan!
The treachery
of saboteurs,
White expertise's
brilliance
outdo
with your inventiveness,
Soviet workers'
millions!
We're Marconis
of giant attainments,
energies,
flights
and lights,
but the thing
we cherish most,
which never will be overshadowed,
is our Land of Soviets,
gaining daily in might,
our Soviet freedom,
our Soviet sunshine,
our Soviet banner.

(1929)

A STORY OF KUZNETSKSTROY
AND ITS BUILDERS

> 1,000,000 waggons of build-
> ing material will be delivered
> here. A giant steel mill, colos-
> sal collieries and a city for
> hundreds of thousands will be
> set up here in five years' time...

(Conversation)

*Translated by
Dorian Rottenberg*

The clouds go roving
through the sky.

The drizzle
               grips the heart.
In cramping damp
               the workers lie
beneath an ancient cart.
Though all is soaked
               both near and far
they whisper,
               anyhow,
"There'll be
               a garden-city here
in just four years
               from now."
Rope-thick,
               the rain
               lays on like whips.
The leaden night's like ink.
With mud
               the workers' clothing drips.
The splinter-torches
               blink.
Their lips
               turn blue as plums with chill,
but whispers every voice:
"That garden-city will be—
               will!
No doubt about it, boys! "
The sodden ground
               steams like hot stew;
poor comfort
               in the wet.
In semi-dark
               the workers chew
the bread-like stuff
               they get.
Yet still
               their whisper one can hear
though loud
               the raindrops fall—
"There'll be a garden-city here
with lights,
               and flowers,
               and all.
The burst and boom of dynamite
will shoo away
               the bear,
while monster-mines
               in quest of coal
the bowels of earth
               will tear.

Pitch high
            the walls
                        of factories!
Let whistles
            wheeze with steam!
With hundred-sun-power furnaces
Siberia
            will gleam.
We'll live in handsome houses
                                    all,
unrationed bread
                        we'll eat
and far beyond
                        old lake Baikal
the scared taiga'll retreat."
The workers'
                whisper
                            grew and grew
above the rain-cloud herds.
And GARDEN-CITY
                        were the two
most clear and frequent words.
That garden
                shall be blooming,
that city must
                    arise
when Soviet Russia
                        has such men
as these before my eyes.

1929

LOVERS OF HARDSHIPS*

Translated by
Dorian Rottenberg

He loves to whisper,
                        cunning and quiet,
in all the cities
                and townships:
"T-ss, gentlemen,
                        they've landed
                                        right
in the middle of some kind of hardships! "
He giggles
                at newspapers,
                                grins over figures:

"Overdone it—
                investing too much in machines!

T-ss, gentlemen,
                    fine—
                              they'll come into bigger
hardships this time,
                    it seems."
He twirls
          his mustachios,
                              merry and smart.
"Their affairs
          have become even worse:
T-ss, gentlemen,
                    wait now—
                                   it's hard
to see how they'll manage
                              not to burst! "
Gathering
          gossips,
                    liars and liaresses,
the gang
          starts discoursing so:
"T-ss, gentlemen,
                    instead of successes
they're suffering hardships!
                              Fine!
                                   Bravo! "
Hardships surmounted,
                         he lowers his tone,
turning
          from glad
                    to sad.
Successes?
          He'll milk them!
                              He won't miss his own,
he's not
          that kind of a lad!
Not only his own share
                         he'll gobble up,
                                        but
he'll bite off
          another's bit,
into every queue
               he's certain to butt,
profiting, too,
               from it.
And as soon as we climb
                         out of dirt and mud
he'll be first to turn up,
                         audacious,
and, beating his chest,
                    will holler out loud:

"My,
                didn't we sweat! Good gracious! "
The republic'll overcome
                        economic misfortunes,
    the foe
            into pulp
                    our gun-butts will beat.
Clear out of our way
                    all the swamp-stuck
                                    flaw-searchers
    muddling
            under
                    our feet!

(1929)

LENINITES*

*Translated by
Dorian Rottenberg*

If
    we weren't
                starved out
                        by blockade,
    nor devoured
            by the wars
                        which we fought,
    it was because
                we followed,
                        we made
    a model of Lenin,
                his word,
                        his thought.

"For the Republic,
                forward
                        charge!
    Let not an enemy
                stay at large! "
    At Lenin's first bidding
                    we rose
                            and hence
    won victory
            in the Republic's defence.
    "Lathe
            and machine-tool
                    and workbench—
                                each

    treble your output
                    our target to reach! "

So
we were bidden
to work
by Ilyich.
"Mine more oil and coal,
make the country rich! "
So we work,
as bade by Ilyich.
"Reduce expenses,
poor quality ditch! "
summons our factory whistles'
screech.
"Harvesters,
onto common land switch,
factories,
lights over wastelands pitch! "
So the Soviets
were bade by Ilyich.
"Save up
in every corner and niche,
to count every kopeck
learn and teach"—
thus to run the economy
called Ilyich.
"With electric lamps
smash darkness's siege,
let their blaze
throughout
the Republic reach."
Thus to light up our life
called Ilyich.
"Religion's opium—
for progress a hitch.
Don't listen to priests
who prattle and preach."
So to live
we were taught by Ilyich.
"Workers,
teach bureaucrats
which is which.
Reach the blighters
under each paper ridge.
Don't treat criticism
as a mad bitch.
Don't fear
it'll make your authority bleach."
So we were taught
to act
by Ilyich.
"From the *left*
don't tear Communism
stich from stich..

On the *right*
>   don't whimper at lowest pitch! "
So to march
>   we were taught by Ilyich.
"Muzzle the fascist!
>   Enough has the midge
attacked us workers
>   with murderous itch."
So we were bade
>   to advance by Ilyich.

Don't whine—
>   better celebrate
>>   Leninism's triumph.
Lenin is with us,
>   undying indeed.
Spreading Universewide,
>   go flying
Lenin's ideas,
>   his word
>>   and his deed.

(1930)

WHAT IS GOOD AND WHAT IS BAD

Translated by
Dorian Rottenberg

One fine day
   a tiny laddie
came
  and asked his dad:
"Could you tell me,
     Daddy,
what is good and what is bad?"
All his daddy said
    I heard.
Children,
   gather near.
Daddy's answer,
     word for word,
I shall tell you
   here.

If the wind
   behaves like mad
bringing hail
   and sleet,
anybody knows
   it's bad—
no walking in the street.

After rainfall
   comes the sun,
driving off the cold.
That is good
   for everyone,
whether young
   or old.

When
  a boy's as black as that—
dirt on cheeks
   and chin,
this is clearly
   very bad
for the youngster's skin.

If a boy
      keeps clean and neat,
washes
      twice a day,
he's a darling,
        simply sweet,
a good lad,
      anyway.

When a bully,
      Tom or Billy,
thrashes
      weaker mates,
his behaviour's bad and silly—
which everybody
        hates.

This one shouts:
      "You mustn't touch
smaller boys
      than you! "
I admire him
      very much,
and so
    I'm sure,
      do you.

If you spoil
      a book and toy
in
 a single day,
"That's a baddish little boy! "
everyone will say.

This one loves
      to work and read,
likes drawing
      in his pad.
He's a good one,
      yes, indeed,
the proper kind
      of lad!

This baby's scared
      to see a crow.
Shame
   upon the lad!
Cowardice,
      you ought to know,
is very,
   very bad.

This one
      shoos the bird away
from a hen and chicks.
Good!
      A brave boy,
                we can say,
though he's hardly six.

This one
      wallows in the dirt,
giggling with joy,
soils his trousers
          and his shirt,
bad,
    untidy boy!

This one
      cleans his shoes himself,
though
      just four years old,
puts his things
        upon a shelf.
He's
   as good as gold!

Remember,
      all who aren't yet big:
if you're now
      a piggy,
you'll become
      a downright pig
when you grow up
        bigger.

Sonny beamed—
        he'd understood
and he told his dad:
"Dad,
    I'll always
      do what's good
and never do
      what's bad! "
(1925)

*Translated by
Avril Pyman*

*English translation
©
Progress Publishers 1978
©
Raduga Publishers 1985

MEET THE BEASTS*

The Lion's neither last nor least,
Come, take a good, hard look.
He's no longer
      King of Beasts,
Just Chairman—in this book.

This animal is called the Lama.
Lama-daughter,
                    Lama-mama.

Two Pelicans in mid-Atlantic
One very small—and one gigantic.

Here's the Zebra—at her nattiest!
Stripier than a garden-mattress.

Now straight into our book there pants
a family
            of
                Elephants.
Two stories' and three stories' tall
With ears like dishes,
And on each face a front-tail called
A "trunk"—a trunk that swishes.
And from their mouths—
                    a fearful sight—
Ivory tusks
            all curving white.
How many new clothes they must need,
What lots to eat and drink!
Their baby grows at such a speed
He'll soon outgrow our dad, I think.
Way, make way, the Elephant
Needs room to wag his head!
A page is really much too cramped!
Give 'em a two-page spread!

Crocodile! The children's dread!
Better not to tease him,
He's skulking on the river-bed,
So no one ever sees him.

Here's a Camel. On the Camel
Loads are carried,
                    people travel.
He lives amongst the desert sands,
Eats nasty-tasting bushes, and,
A beast of burden,
                    strong
                        and sound,
Is hard at work the whole year round.

The Kangaroo.
                Such a funny old sport!
Her arms are twice as short.
But, to make up,
                    her strong
Back legs are twice as long!

Father Giraffe
has a long neck—
it's
A problem to get him a collar that fits.

Giraffes are lucky:
the mother giraffe's
Got plenty
of neck for
the cuddliest calf.

The Monkey.
Funniest of the lot.
Sits like a statue, still as he can!
If not for that tail he's got,
He might be posing as a man!
In wintertime this beast feels blue
The poor beast's from the tropic zone.
But, now I've seen the lot of you,
Good-bye, nice beasts—time I went home!

(1926)

WHAT SHALL I BE?*

Translated by
Dorian Rottenberg

Time gets along, and I grow up;
I'm seventeen next year.
What shall I choose—
what sort of job
to start
on my career?

Carpenters are clever folk.
Making furniture's no joke;
we take
a big, round log,
first thing,
and to a bench
the log we bring.
Now we saw it—
like that! —
into planks,
long and flat.
After working such a lot
the busy saw
becomes red-hot.
Round about the sawdust flies—
there in yellow heaps it lies.

Now
       we take a plane
and set to work again.
Back and forth,
          to and fro—
off the knots and snags all go.
If we need
       a ball or knob
a lathe is used
         to do the job.
One by one we make the parts,
then the work of joining starts.
Wardrobe, armchair,
          table, chest—
neat and strong—
        the very best!

Making furniture is good
yet building is no worse.
I'd be a builder, yes, I would,
just let them teach me first.
I'd make a drawing
         for a start
of a house
       that's to my heart.
What the builders have to do
is make the house look fine,
spacious, handsome,
         nice and new,
windows all ashine!
Here's the front—
it's called *façade;*   .
there
      the garden will be laid.
Here we'll have a gravel path,
there the pantry and the bath.
The drawing's finished.
         You and I
and all the rest get busy.
The scaffolding goes up sky-high;
to look down makes you dizzy.
Where
      the work's too hard for man
cranes and pulleys
         lend a hand;
steel girders
        they hoist up like sticks
together with
        whole piles of bricks.

We lay tin sheet upon the roof
to make it strong
                    and waterproof.
The house is ready,
                    spacious, tall,
and beautiful to see.
There's room enough in it for all
for every family.

It's good to be a builder,
but a doctor's job's no worse.
I'd gladly cure sick children,
just let them teach me first.
I'd go to Pete,
I'd go to Bill:
"Hello there, boys!
Now, who is ill?
Stick your tongue out—
right you are—
that's the spirit—
                    now say *A-A-h!*
Put this thermometer
                    under your tongue.
Don't be afraid,
                    you won't get stung! "
I'll ask little Bill
to swallow a pill
and give powders to Pete;
each and every I'll treat!
I'll tell little Ned
to stay in bed
till he's healthy again
and forgets his pain!
With a pat on his tummy
I'll turn to his Mummy
and give her prescriptions
                    for medicine drops.
I'll tell her they ought to
be taken in water
three times a day
                    till the fever stops.

Of course, a doctor's job is good,
but a worker's is no worse.
I'd be a worker, yes, I would,
just let them teach me first.
Now, stir up, lad
                    it's time to go!
Can't you hear the whistle blow?
To the factory we come,
I and Timothy, my chum.

Some jobs
        are much too hard
                for one.
Together, though, we'll get them done.
Mighty scissors go snip-snip,
cutting iron,
          strip by strip.
Cranes go rolling,
huge loads hauling.
Steam-presses pat
steel ingots flat.
Driving lathes
         or smelting metal—
every job takes skill and mettle,
and nobody can boast
that his is needed most.
I'll make an iron nut,
          and you
forge a tightly-fitting screw.
Then the work of each,
           non-stop,
goes to the assembly-shop.
Every screw
       gets in its hole,
fixing parts
       into one whole.
The rafters shake,
such a noise we make.
Thunder,
     lightning,
almost frightening!
And now an engine,
         huge and strong,
rolls out
     to pull a train along.

It's jolly good,
        a factory,
but a tram-car is no worse.
A conductor's
        is the job for me,
just let them teach me first.
Conductors!
        Aren't they lucky chaps!
With great big bags
        on leather straps,
everywhere
       and all day long
in their trams
       they ride along,
selling tickets to us all:

parents, children,
                    big and small,
tickets yellow,
                    blue and red
for me, for you,
                    for Pete and Ned.
Along rails we ride
through the traffic tide.
Now the rails have ended;
get out,
            everyone!
Isn't it splendid,
                    the woods,
                                the sun!

A conductor's job is good,
but a driver's is no worse.
I'd be a car-driver, I would,
just let them teach me first.
Purr along,
              my motor-car;
on and on we glide.
It's wonderful
                how fast and far
A motor-car can ride.
Only say
            where to,
                        which way—
home I'll drive you
                        straightaway!
Hoot-toot-toot,
                  I blow the horn.
"Don't get in the way! "
                          I warn.

A driver's job is pretty good,
but a pilot's is no worse.
I'd be a pilot,
                yes, I would,
just let them teach me first.
I fill the fuel-tanks
                      to the top,
the engine starts to roar.
Fly me,
        engine,
                  up and up,
where the eagles soar!
It doesn't matter
                    if we meet

rain or snow
                        or hail and sleet—
up we go above the clouds
gathering in fluffy crowds!
Like the birds
                my plane and I
over seas and oceans fly.
Drive me, engine, to the moon,
a planet and a star,
although I know how very far
the stars and planets are!

It's true, a pilot's job is good,
but is a sailor's worse?
I'd be a sailor-lad,
                        I would,
just let them teach me first!
My sailor-hat's
                got ribbon-tails,
there's anchors
                on my sleeves;
from coast to coast
                my steamer sails
across the seven seas!
The waves leap high,
                        the billows toss,
all roaring angrily.
But I just skim
                across their tops,
no waves too high for me!
Calm down,
            mad tempest,
                        shut your mouth,
give up, wind,
            and don't wail!
I'll reach the Poles,
                both North and South,
in spite of any gale!

And now my story's told at last,
I hope you've understood:
choose any job
                that suits your taste,
for any job
            is good!

(1928)

UNFINISHED

I*

*Translated by
Peter Tempest*

She loves me? Loves me not? My hands I'm wringing
the knuckles as they crack
                              I throw around
like petals luckless lovers pluck
                                    in springtime
from ox-eye daisies by the pathway found
what if my hair prove grey when I am shorn
And silver as the years go by
                                more plentiful
I hope I trust the day shall never dawn
when I stoop to the shame of being sensible

IV**

*Translated by
Irina Zheleznova*

It's after one and you must be in bed. Uncurbed,
The Milky Way flows through the night, a silver stream.
No telegrams, a thunderbolt each one, I'll not disturb
You, that's a promise. Sleep and have your dreams.
Its over. Period. The love boat's smashed
against the reefs of day-to-day existence.
We're quits, so why keep score of all the rash
things said and done with such perverse insistence!
How still the world is! See? Night from the skies
Exacts a tribute: stars. Filled with elation,
It's then one wants to rise—rise and address
Time, time and history, and all creation...

V*

*Translated by
Peter Tempest*

I know the force of words and warning they can sound
I don't mean those which draw front-row applause
But words at which coffins break loose to pound
the ground this way and that with heavy paws
They may be cast out publishers ignore them
But words forge on tighten their belly-bands
ring through the centuries and trains come crawling
to lick and fondle poetry's horny hands
I know the force of words They seem a petal flung
Under the heels of dancers just a trifle
But man possesses backbone heart and tongue

*English translation
©
Raduga Publishers 1985
**English translation
©
Raduga Publishers 1984

(1928–1930)

NOTES

I MYSELF

1 Mayakovsky wrote his autobiography "I Myself" in 1922. He brought it up to date six years later, in 1928.

The autobiography is written in a semi-humorous tone and is polemical in many respects.

WHAT MATTERS

2 Mayakovsky was born on 7 (19) July 1893 in the village of Bagdady, now Mayakovsky in the Georgian SSR.

1st RECOLLECTION

3 *allongs englong de lar per three*—a punning travesty of the first line of *La Marseillaise, Allons enfants de la patrie.*

1905

4 *the Rion,* or Rioni—a river near Kutaisi.

5 *...General Alikhanov had been assassinated*—a slip on Mayakovsky's part. General Alikhanov was assassinated by revolutionaries in 1907.

SOCIALISM

6 *Burevestnik,* a publishing house that specialized in social-democratic literature.

7 *"Down with the Social-Democrats",* ... *"Chats on Economics"*—those were propaganda pamphlets: the first was written by V. Brakke, the second by N. Koryshev.

8 *...the Erfurt Programme*—the programme of the German Social-Democratic Party, adopted in Erfurt at a congress in 1891; it was studied in Russian revolutionary circles.

REACTION

9 *...in memory of Bauman*—N. E. Bauman was a leading member of the Russian revolutionary movement. He was assassinated in Moscow in 1905.

WORK

10 *...Bem glassware*—E. M. Bem was a fashionable woman artist of that time who painted water-colours in pseudo-Russian folk style; also engaged in glass-painting.

READING

11 *...more than Marx's "Preface"*—a preface to *To the Critique of Political Economy,* written by K. Marx in 1859.

12 *...a dark-blue Two Tactics by Lenin*—V. I. Lenin's book *Two Tactics of Social Democracy in the Democratic Revolution,* written in 1905.

THE PARTY

13 *Took an exam...* Mayakovsky had been doing errands for the Party.

ARREST

14 ...*read Sanin* – the novel by M. P. Artsybashev which had a lurid reputation in those years.

15 ...*And a brief spell inside once more* – Mayakovsky was arrested for the second time on 18 January 1909 and held in custody for over a month.

16 ...*the Crosses* – a current term for the prison; from the shape of the building in Petersburg.

THIRD ARREST

17 ...*the Taganka* – the Taganskaya Prison.

18 *Butyrki* – the Butyrskaya Prison.

11 BUTYRSKY MONTHS

19 *P. Kurlov* – in those years, Deputy Minister of Internal Affairs.

20 ...*sentenced me on the first charge* – the affair of the clandestine printing-press.

A SO-CALLED DILEMMA

21 ...*from the Stroganovsky* – the Stroganovsky Art College.

THE LAST COLLEGE

22 *Sat on my "head" for a year* – that is, learned how to draw human heads.

23 *M. F. Larionov, I. I. Mashkov* – artists.

IN THE SMOKING-ROOM

24 *Isle of the Dead* – a reference to the symphonic work of that name by Sergei Rachmaninov.

A MOST MEMORABLE NIGHT

25 *Russian futurism was born* – futurism as a trend had emerged earlier in Russia. Mayakovsky is referring here to the organization of a group known as the cubo-futurists. Appearing in public with the futurists and publishing his verse in futurist publications, he saw the movement as a force struggling with the mores and art of the bourgeois society and regarded it as innovative. In fact, futurism as an artistic trend reflected the general crisis of bourgeois culture. Although Mayakovsky was associated with futurism, his poetry, with its tragic interpretation of life, its growing social protest and its humanist message, was fundamentally different from that being written by the futurists.

AND SO EVERY DAY

26 *"The white and the crimson..."* – the opening words of the poem "Night".

THE WONDERFUL BURLYUK

27 ...*took me to his place at Novaya Mayachka* – an estate in Kherson Gubernia; D. D. Burlyuk's father was the manager.

28 *Brought "Harbour"...* – one of Mayakovsky's earlier poems.

A SLAP IN THE FACE

29 ...*joint manifesto* – foreword to the collection, *A Slap in the Face of the Public Taste,* published in 1913.

WINTER

30 *"Ah, close, close the eyes of the papers"*—from Mayakovsky's poem "Mother and the Evening Killed by the Germans".

KUOKKALA

31 *...seven dining acquaintances*—while staying at Kuokkala, Mayakovsky often visited the writer K. I. Chukovsky, the director N. I. Yevreinov and the artist I. E. Repin.

32 *...Repin's herbs*—the artist I. E. Repin was a vegetarian.

THE NEW SATIRIKON

33 *The New Satirikon* was a popular satirical weekly magazine of the time.

CALL-UP

34 *They've called me up*. Mayakovsky was called up for army service in October 1915 and posted to the Military Automobile School in Petrograd.

26 FEBRUARY 1917

35 *It's Guchkovizing*—a reference to the establishment of a reactionary political course (named after A. I. Guchkov, Army and Navy Minister in the Provisional Government).

AUGUST

36 *Novaya zhizn* (New Life)—a newspaper in which Mayakovsky appeared for some time.

1918

37 *Dropped in on Kshesinskaya at Proletkult*—Proletkult (then the Society of Proletarian Arts) was accommodated in the former palace of the court ballerina, Kshesinskaya.

25 OCTOBER 1918

38 *M. F. Andreyeva*—an actress at the Moscow Art Theatre and at that time in charge of the Theatre Department of the Petrograd Soviet.

1919

39 *...they are organizing a komfut*—a reference to the foundation of an association of Communist-futurists. *Iskusstvo kommuny* (Art of the Commune), a weekly newspaper published in Petrograd from December 1918 to March 1919.

40 *Have started agitation work for ROSTA*. ROSTA—abbreviation for Russian Telegraph Agency, forerunner of TASS.

1920

41 *Days and nights at ROSTA*—from autumn 1919 to January 1921, Mayakovsky did a great deal of work on propaganda posters.

1923

42 *LEF*—the Left Front of Arts—the name of a literary group and magazine run by Mayakovsky. The magazine came out during the period 1923 to 1925. Mayakovsky tried to unite the members of LEF on a platform of communist ideology with the creation of a revolutionary art as its message. In spite of the definiteness of Mayakovsky's basic positions, the magazine gave space to the erroneous vulgar-sociological and formalist theories of the LEF group.

In 1927, a magazine *Novy LEF* (New LEF) began to come out with Mayakovsky as an editor. In the middle of 1928, Mayakovsky left the LEF group, believing that "petty literary factions had played themselves out". Explaining his departure from LEF, Mayakovsky said that it was "an aesthetic group which had taken up our struggle as a fact and had turned revolutionary literature into a self-contained aesthetic enterprise".

1927

43 *I am reviving... LEF, now "New"*—a reference to the magazine *Novy Lef,* which came out under Mayakovsky's editorship from 1927 to 1928.

1928

44 *I am writing a poem "Bad"*—it was not, in fact, ever written.

45 *A play*—a reference to *The Bedbug,* finished in the second half of that year.

I

46 *...Shustov's works...*—N. L. Shustov—owner of wine distilleries.

47 *...shopwindows at Avanzo's*—art-salon on Kuznetsky Most, a fashionable street in Moscow.

48 *I like to watch how little children die...*—in some of his early poems Mayakovsky masquerades as a ruffian and cynic. His attempts to shock the reader with audacious, unusual statements and buffoonery running counter to common morality, are intended to conceal his tragic view of life. Hence, as the poet pointed out himself, these words should not be understood literally.

YOU!

49 *...crooning Severyanin*—I. V. Severyanin, poet-decadent, active participant of the futurist movement in Russia. His poems, distinguished by quaint mannerisms and extravagance of wording, enjoyed noisy success among petty-bourgeois audiences.

TO ALL AND EVERYTHING

50 *...the face of Razin*—Stepan Razin—leader of peasant uprising in late seventeenth century Russia, executed after the uprising was crushed.

LILY DEAR! IN LIEU OF A LETTER

51 Dedicated to Lily Brik with whom Mayakovsky became acquainted in summer 1915.

52 *Kruchonykh's Inferno*—allusion to "Games in Hell", a futurist poem by A. Kruchonykh and V. Khlebnikov (1919).

FED UP

53 *I. F. Annensky, F. I. Tyutchev, A. A. Fet*—19th century lyric poets.

54 *Plain as Mooing*—one of Mayakovsky earliest collections.

REVOLUTION (A POET'S CHRONICLE)

55 *...the dome of the Duma*—dome of Tavrichesky Palace in Petrograd which housed the State Duma—an elective body of parliamentary type which existed in Russia in 1906-1917, having purely consultative functions.

56 *...Petropavlovskaya's bastions*—bastions of Sts. Peter and Paul Fortress in Petrograd, situated on one of the islands of the River Neva.

ORDER OF THE DAY TO THE ARMY OF ARTS

57 *Futurists, leave off waddling, lame...*—after the victory of the October Revolution, futurists, intending to co-operate with the new

administration, took active part in the work of some government bodies concerned with cultural affairs, e. g., certain departments of Narkompros (People's Commissariat for Public Education), as well as newspapers *Iskusstvo kommuny* (Art of the Commune) and magazines. Mayakovsky, who at that time believed the futurists' activities to be best adjusted to the requirements of the new era, calls on them to step up their fight against "the old"—the customs, traditions and cultural heritage of the past.

With time, Mayakovsky's attitude to futurism, its importance and role in art, underwent considerable changes.

[58] *No sovdep'll make armies go anywhere...* —sovdep—composite abbreviation of two words: Soviet (council) and deputies, meaning Council of Workers', Peasants' and Soldiers' Deputies.

LEFT MARCH (FOR SAILORS)

[59] On March 25, 1930, speaking at Krasnaya Presnya Komsomol Club, Mayakovsky recounted the way this poem came into being: "I received a phonecall from the former Naval Guard Headquarters demanding me to come and read poetry, and so, sitting in a cab, I wrote 'Left March'. Of course, some of the stanzas had been ready before, so here I simply joined into one whole the lines addressed to sailors."

[60] *Mauser*—type of pistol named after inventor.

[61] *...under the Entente*—Entente cordiale—imperialist alliance, conducted intervention against the young Soviet republic.

AN AMAZING ADVENTURE OF VLADIMIR MAYAKOVSKY

[62] *...about the beastly ROSTA...*—ROSTA—see Note 40.

ROT

[63] *...without the hammer and sickle...*—official symbols of the Soviet State depicted on the emblems of the USSR and constituent republics.

[64] *Worse than Wrangel...*—General Wrangel, who commanded the White Army at the very end of the Civil War, established a military dictatorship in the Crimea and Southern Ukraine.

ORDER NO. 2 TO THE ARMY OF ARTS

[65] *proletcultists*—members of Proletcult (abbreviation from "proletarian culture")—a cultural and educational society organized in September 1917 for the development of amateur art among workers. Renouncing the classical heritage, proletcultist theoreticians spread the erroneous view that a "purely proletarian" culture could be created by so-called "laboratory methods". The proletcultist doctrine was sharply criticized by V. I. Lenin.

CONFERENCE-CRAZY

[66] This poem was highly estimated by V. I. Lenin at a meeting of the Communist group of the All-Russia Congress of Metalworkers, March 6, 1922. In his speech devoted to the international and domestic situation of the Soviet Republic, he said the following: "Yesterday I happened to read in *Izvestia* a political poem by Mayakovsky. I am not an admirer of his poetical talent, although I admit that I am not a competent judge. But I have not for a long time read anything on politics and administration with so much pleasure as I read this. In his poem he derides this meeting habit, and taunts the Communists with incessantly sitting at meetings. I am not sure about the poetry; but as for the politics, I vouch for their absolute correctness." (V. I. Lenin, *Collected Works*, Vol. 33, p. 223).

WE DON'T BELIEVE

67 ...*million-strong* RCP—Russian Communist Party.

UNIVERSAL REPLY

68 This poem appeared in response to the British Government's note delivered on May 8, 1923.

VOROVSKY

69 Written in connection with the murder in Lausanne on May 10, 1923, of Vatslav Vorovsky, a prominent figure in the Communist Party, then Soviet Ambassador to Italy.

JUBILEE POEM

70 *Look at that...* —Mayakovsky points to a huge poster which at that time, in 1924, stood prominently in Tverskoy Boulevard near the Pushkin monument. It showed a blue lump of sugar with bright rays radiating from it—the "ginger moustache".

71 *...tougher than Poltava...* —Battle of Poltava between Russian army led by Peter the Great, and Swedish forces, described in Alexander Pushkin's poem "Poltava".

72 *Die-hard Plyushkin...* —proverbial miser, character in Gogol's *Dead Souls.*

73 *Gavrila Derzhavin* —Russian poet of 18th-early 19th century.

74 *A prisoner of honour... by a bullet slain...* —quote from Mikhail Lermontov's poem "On the Death of a Poet" (on the death of Pushkin).

VLADIKAVKAZ-TIFLIS

75 *Vladikavkaz* —city in the Caucasus, now Ordzhonikidze;*Tiflis*—capital of Georgia, now Tbilisi.

76 *I'm a Georgian born*—the poet was born in the village of Bagdady, now called Mayakovsky, in the Georgian SSR, the Caucasus.

77 *Elbrus, Kazbek* —Caucasian mountains.

78 *arkhaluk* —Caucasian dress without fasteners.

79 *Daryal* —canyon in the Caucasus, valley of the River Terek.

80 *musháh* (Georg.) —farm labourer.

81 *Shota Rustaveli* —great Georgian poet of the twelfth century, contemporary of Queen Tamara.

82 *saklya* —Caucasian dwelling made of stone or bricks.

83 *...golden shoulderstrapped Russians*—allusion to detachments of Russian troops engaged in suppressing popular uprisings in mid-nineteenth century Georgia against social and national oppression.

84 *"Mkholot shen erts ratz, rom chemtvis, Moutsia maglidgan gmerts..."* (Georg.)—"To you alone I give all I received from God on high."

85 *...as Arsen the Avenger*—Arsen Georgiashvili—participant of revolutionary events in 1905, executed in 1906 for assassinating a general of the Russian Tsar's Army.

86 *Alikhanov's whiplash scream...* M. Alikhanov-Avarsky—Russian tsarist general, governor-general of Kutais Gubernia, Georgia; assassinated in 1907.

87 *madchari* (Georg.)—young wine.

88 *kinto* (Georg.)—travelling trader, joker, mischief-maker.

89 *...zurna-like...* —zurna—Georgian national wind instrument.

90 *shairi* (Georg.)—poetry.

TAMARA AND THE DEMON

[91] *Tamara*–Georgian queen, figuring in many legends as well as works of literature and art.

[92] *...as drunken Esenin...*–allusion to the poet's bohemian lifestyle in the twenties.

[93] *As if Lunacharsky had organized the Terek...*–jocular allusion to Anatoly Lunacharsky (1875-1933), prominent Soviet cultural worker, always extremely active and full of energy, simultaneously engaged in most widely different activities, which at times had no connection whatever with his main duties as People's Commissar of Education.

[94] *P. S. Kogan*–critic and literary historian, a worker in the People's Commissariat for Education.

[95] *...having got information from Lermontov...*–Tamara is one of the main characters in Lermontov's poem *The Demon*.

[96] *...one of the chaps I knew...*–Mayakovsky implies Boris Pasternak, a Soviet poet, whose book *My Sister, Life* includes a poem called "In Memory of the Demon".

FROM POEMS DEVOTED TO PARIS

[97] In November-December 1924 Mayakovsky travelled to France. Impressions from this trip gave rise to a cycle of poems about Paris.

THE CITY

[98] *...and no Herriot...*–Eduard Herriot in 1924-1925 headed the French Government.

[99] "Un verre de Koto donne de l'energie" (Fr.)–"One sip of Koto brings new energy".

[100] *fellow-traveller*–reference to writers of non-proletarian origin who nevertheless accepted the Revolution. In the conditions of the ideological and esthetic battles and literary polemics of the period, the term was often applied rather arbitrarily.

VERLAINE AND CEZANNE

[101] *Pauline Garcia Viardaux*–French singer, intimate friend of Ivan Turgenev.

[102] *Rudin*–main character of Turgenev's novel of the same name.

[103] *"Comment ça va, cher camarade Verlaine?"* (Fr.)–"How do you do, dear comrade Verlaine?"

[104] *..."Face about to the countryside"*–one of the slogans of the twenties, orienting literary workers towards depiction of peasant life and processes taking place in the countryside. Mayakovsky's irony is spearheaded against those who understood the slogan too primitively and literally.

[105] *GUS*–State Scientific Council of the RSFSR People's Commissariat for Public Education.

[106] *I. V. Vardin* (Mcheladze)–literary critic, many of whose articles were written in peremptory style.

[107] *AKhRR*–Artists' Association of Revolutionary Russia.

[108] *La Rotonde*–name of a café in Paris.

VERSAILLES

[109] *Capet*–dynastic name of Louis XVI dethroned in 1792.

[110] *...for their Pompadours...*–Marquise de Pompadour was a favourite of Louis XV.

[111] *sans-culottes* (Fr.)–pantless–nickname of revolutionaries in France.

FAREWELL (AT A CAFE)

[112] *A Chekist*—member of Cheka—security forces.

FROM POEMS ABOUT AMERICA

[113] In 1925 Mayakovsky made a trip to America. After a short stay in Paris, he sailed on board a steamer to Mexico. After a while in Mexico, he received a visa for entry into the United States, where in the course of three months he visited a number of major cities. The impressions from this trip were used in a cycle of poems written in 1925-26, part of which are included in this edition. Many of the names, facts and events reflected in this cycle are also mentioned in *My Discovery of America*, a series of essays written by Mayakovsky at the same time.

ATLANTIC OCEAN

[114] *Revkom*—revolutionary committees, sprung up spontaneously in October 1917 as headquarters of local uprisings.

[115] CEC—Central Executive Committee—functioned as a supreme state body in the intervals between Congresses of Soviets.

SOME SHALLOW PHILOSOPHY OVER THE DEEPS

[116] *Yu. M. Steklov*—editor of newspaper *Izvestia TsIK*, where he regularly published extremely long articles. In this case Mayakovsky's irony is directed at the abundance of vacuous periods, "a lot of water", as they say.

[117] *Demyan Bedny* (1883-1945)—a well-known Soviet poet.

[118] The Russian for whale-bone is a word meaning whiskers.

BLACK AND WHITE

[119] *Antonio Maceo*—Cuban national hero.

MEXICO

[120] *bulldog*—vernacular for revolver; in this instance a toy pistol.

[121] *LEF*—magazine of the Left Front of Arts (1923-1925), whose editor-in-chief was Mayakovsky. During his trips abroad the poet usually took numerous copies of the magazine in order to acquaint progressive-minded readers with it.

[122] *Montiguomo Hawk Talon* and Pale-Faced Brother—nicknames of gymnasium pupils enthusiastic about novels about Indians; the said pupils are characters in A. P. Chekhov's story "Boys".

[123] *Gringoes and Gachupinoes*—contemptuous nicknames for Americans and Spaniards in Mexico.

[124] *pulke*—alcoholic drink.

[125] *Hernando Cortés*—fifteenth century Spanish conqueror.

[126] *Moctezuma*—the last Aztec king who betrayed his people.

[127] *Guatemoc*—leader of the Aztecs.

[128] *Porfirio Diaz, Victoriano Huerta*—presidents of Mexico.

[129] *serape*—national costume; *guadeloupe*—textile from which it is made.

[130] *Chapultepek*—garden and square in Mexico City.

[131] *Emiliano Zapata*—leader of peasants in Mexican Civil War in the early twentieth century.

[132] *Galvana, Moreno, Carillo*—Mexican revolutionaries.

A SKYSCRAPER DISSECTED

133 *Yelets or Konotop*—small provincial towns in pre-revolutionary Russia, synonymous of stagnation.

134 *Coolidge*—30th President of the USA in 1923-29.

A DECENT CITIZEN

135 *NEP*—New economic policy, conducted in the USSR in 1921-1929, aimed at restoring and developing the national economy destroyed during the Civil War. NEP offered a certain freedom of activity for private enterprise, which led to a revival of bourgeois tendencies in the country. This situation had an adverse effect on the revolutionary enthusiasm of certain participants of the recent struggle against the tsar, which is indirectly alluded to in this poem.

136 *Father Platón*—priest of Russian Orthodox Church in New York.

HOME!

137 *Gosplan*—State Planning Committee of the USSR, carries out long- and short-term economic planning.

TO SERGEI ESENIN

138 *...poor class-contact*—contact with the masses—a slogan widespread in the twenties, addressed to art workers, calling them to establish firm ties with the broad working masses. Such ties were considered a reliable guarantee against erroneous behaviour and ideas. Mayakovsky ridiculed the vulgarization of this concept.

139 *kvass* (Russ.)—popular non-alcoholic beverage.

140 *...by someone "at the post"*—*Na postu* (At the Post)—magazine, mouthpiece of one of the leading literary groupings of the twenties, the Russian Association of Proletarian Writers (RAPP).

141 *Nikolai Doronin*—poet, contemporary of Mayakovsky.

142 *Leonid Sobinov*—famous tenor who sang at the Esenin memorial meeting in the Moscow Art Theatre.

143 *Not a word, my friend, not a sigh*—initial words of a romance by Tchaikovsky to the words by Pleshcheyev.

144 Loengrin's part in Wagner's opera was considered one of Sobinov's finest.

145 *P. S. Kogan*—Soviet critic, target of many sarcastic quips on the part of Mayakovsky (see Note 94).

146 *Dying in this life is not so hard, building life is harder, I daresay*—paraphrase of Esenin's lines: "Dying in this life is not so new, yet living, certainly, is not much newer."

TO BRITISH WORKERS

147 Written in connection with the general strike of British workers on May 4-12 1926, printed in a newspaper with the note:
"I donate the money for this poem to the Striking Fund and challenge my comrades-poets to do the same. Vl. M."

148 *...the dawn of our Revolution*—the date of the Great October Socialist Revolution in Russia is October 25 (November 7) 1917.

BRIBE-TAKERS

149 *GUM*—Central Department Store in Moscow, one of the biggest of its kind.

150 *...October's glow*—October is synonymous to the Great October Socialist Revolution.

151 *...I could give a White Guard my hand...*—White Guard (opposite to Red Guard)—member of the counter-revolutionary forces in the Civil War.

A MESSAGE TO PROLETARIAN POETS

[152] *Alexander Bezymensky* (1898-1973), *Mikhail Svetlov* (1903-64), *Iosif Utkin* (1903-44)–Soviet poets, Mayakovsky's contemporaries.

A FACTORY OF BUREAUCRATS

[153] *...pre-February eagle-bearing buttons*–a hint at bureaucracy, which, undermining the gains of the October Revolution, stimulated the restoration of capitalist ways: the coat-tails of the tsar's officials were embossed with buttons bearing the image of the two-headed eagle, the symbol of the monarchy overthrown by the Bourgeois-Democratic revolution of February 1917.

TO COMRADE NETTE–STEAMER AND MAN

[154] *Theodore Nette*–Soviet diplomatic courier, died a hero's death in February 1926 in a train carriage travelling through Latvia, defending diplomatic mail against an attack by agents of foreign secret services. The name of Nette was given to a steamship of the Black Sea Merchant Fleet, which Mayakovsky saw in summer 1926 in the Odessa Harbour.

[155] *Roman Yakobson*–philologist, Mayakovsky's and Nette's friend.

PAPERWORK HABITS

[156] *Put me in Rykov's place for an hour...*–A. I. Rykov–head of security forces at the time.

TO OUR YOUNG GENERATION

[157] *...as if you were listening to MKHAT*–the Moscow Academic Art Theatre was long considered to offer a standard of correct Russian pronunciation.

[158] *mazanki*–Ukrainian cottages, before the Revolution usually built of reeds stuccoed with clay.

[159] *Ingushes, Ossetins*–Caucasian nationalities.

[160] *Khokhol*–nickname for a Ukrainian.

[161] *"Ne chuyu"* (Ukr.)–"I don't understand".

[162] *Katsap*–nickname for a Russian.

[163] *Russopets*–in this case, Russians flaunting their exaggerated national merits.

MY BEST POEM

[164] *...the workers and troops of Canton have occupied Shanghai...*–during the revolutionary Civil War in China in 1914-27, Canton (a city in Southern China) was the seat of an antiimperialist government whose troops in March 1927 helped to liberate Shanghai from the militarists.

YEKATERINBURG-SVERDLOVSK

[165] *Yekaterinburg*–former name of Sverdlovsk, major industrial city in the Urals, centre of an area of diverse mining and other enterprises.

[166] *...like Kate the Great...*–Catherine II–Empress of Russia.

[167] *Kolchak*–commander-in-chief of White armies in Siberia and the Urals during the Civil War; *Gaida*–leader of counter-revolutionary Czech Corps.

OFFICE-BUGS

[168] *MKK*–Moscow Control Commission–carried out the functions of Party control.

THE COWARD

169 *RKI*—Workers' and Peasants' Inspection, endowed with functions of public control.

170 *mestkom*—TU local committee.

171 *domkom*—house committee, usually established in apartment houses to supervise different local affairs and maintain public order.

LINES NOT ON BIG BUT PETTY TRASH...

172 *IWH*—International Workers' Help.

YOUTH'S SECRET

173 *K. I. M.*—Communist Youth International.

THE PILLAR

174 *Sovnarkom*—Council of People's Commissars, equivalent to Council of Ministers.

THE GOSSIP

175 *Sorokin*—from Russian *soroka*—magpie.

176 *Gubcommittee*—regional committee, from *gubernia* which means region.

A LETTER FROM PARIS TO COMRADE KOSTROV...

177 *T. Kostrov*—then editor of the newspaper *Komsomolskaya pravda*.

A LETTER TO TATYANA YAKOVLEVA

178 *T. A. Yakovleva*, the letter's addressee, since 1925 lived abroad, in Paris, where she emigrated at her father's insistence. Mayakovsky got acquainted with her in 1926 during his trip to Paris.

ALL'S QUIET IN THE WEST

179 *basmaches*—participants of subversive bands which in the twenties conducted armed struggle against Soviet power in the Central Asian republics.

180 *August the First*—International Anti-War Day celebrated at that time.

REQUEST TO READERS

Raduga Publishers would be glad
to have your opinion of this
book, its translation and design
and any suggestions you may
have for future publications.
Please send all your comments
to 21, Zubovsky Boulevard,
Moscow, USSR.

ИБ № 1650
Редактор русского текста *А. А. Кудряшова*
Контрольный редактор *Л. Д. Киржнер*
Художник *В. И. Чистяков*
Художественный редактор *Т. В. Иващенко*
Технический редактор *В. Н. Гунина*

Сдано в набор 4.10.84. Подписано в печать 11.05.85.
Формат 60x84/16. Бумага офсетная.
Гарнитура Пресс-Роман. Печать офсетная.
Усл. печ. л. 16,27 + 1,39 печ. л. вклеек. Усл. кр.-отт. 21,99.
Уч.-изд. л. 21,4. Тираж 13920 экз. Заказ № 1094.
Цена 2 р. 80 к. Изд. № 31.

Издательство ''Радуга'' Государственного комитета СССР
по делам издательств, полиграфии и книжной торговли.
Москва, 119859, Зубовский бульвар, 17.

Отпечатано с оригинал-макета методом фотоофсет
на Можайском полиграфкомбинате Союзполиграфпрома
при Государственном комитете СССР по делам
издательств, полиграфии и книжной торговли.
Можайск, 143200, ул. Мира, 93.